Retro Kid

RETROKIDPUBLISHING.COM

👉 **DISTILLER:** . . . .

AGE/EXPRESSION: . . . .

ORIGIN: . . . .   **PRICE:** . . . .

SAMPLED: . . . .   **RATING:** ☆ ☆ ☆ ☆ ☆

COLOR METER: FLAVOR WHEEL:

COLOR METER:
- MAHOGANY
- CARAMEL
- AMBER
- GOLD
- HONEY
- STRAW
- CLEAR

FLAVOR WHEEL:

HEAT/ %
ABV: . . . .

BALANCE   FINISH
BODY   0.5   DARK FRUIT
0.4
ASTRIN-   0.3   CITRUS
GENT   0.2   FRUIT
SALTY   0.1   FLORAL
SWEET   SPICY
SMOKE   HERBAL/
GRASSY
PEAT   MALT/
TOFFEE   CEREAL

NOTES:
. . . .
. . . .
. . . .
. . . .
. . . .
. . . .

👉 DISTILLER: . . . .

AGE/EXPRESSION: . . . .

ORIGIN: . . . . PRICE: . . . .

SAMPLED: . . . . RATING: ☆ ☆ ☆ ☆ ☆

COLOR METER:

- MAHOGANY
- CARAMEL
- AMBER
- GOLD
- HONEY
- STRAW
- CLEAR

FLAVOR WHEEL:

HEAT/ _____ %
ABV: _____

BALANCE · FINISH · DARK FRUIT · CITRUS FRUIT · FLORAL · SPICY · HERBAL/GRASSY · MALT/CEREAL · TOFFEE · PEAT · SMOKE · SWEET · SALTY · ASTRIN-GENT · BODY

0.5 · 0.4 · 0.3 · 0.2 · 0.1

NOTES:

. . . .
. . . .
. . . .
. . . .
. . . .
. . . .

👉 **DISTILLER:** ....

AGE/EXPRESSION: ....

ORIGIN: .... **PRICE:** ....

SAMPLED: .... **RATING:** ☆ ☆ ☆ ☆ ☆

COLOR METER:

MAHOGANY

CARAMEL

AMBER

GOLD

HONEY

STRAW

CLEAR

FLAVOR WHEEL:

HEAT/ABV: _____ %

BALANCE
FINISH
BODY
DARK FRUIT
ASTRIN-GENT
CITRUS FRUIT
SALTY
FLORAL
SWEET
SPICY
SMOKE
HERBAL/GRASSY
PEAT
TOFFEE
MALT/CEREAL

0.1 0.2 0.3 0.4 0.5

NOTES:

....
....
....
....
....
....

👉 **DISTILLER:** ....

AGE/EXPRESSION: ....

ORIGIN: .... **PRICE:** ....

SAMPLED: .... **RATING:** ☆ ☆ ☆ ☆ ☆

COLOR METER:

MAHOGANY

CARAMEL

AMBER

GOLD

HONEY

STRAW

CLEAR

FLAVOR WHEEL:

HEAT/ABV: _____ %

BALANCE

FINISH

BODY

DARK FRUIT

ASTRIN-GENT

CITRUS FRUIT

SALTY

FLORAL

SWEET

SPICY

SMOKE

HERBAL/GRASSY

PEAT

TOFFEE

MALT/CEREAL

0.5
0.4
0.3
0.2
0.1

NOTES:

....

....

....

....

....

....

DISTILLER: ....

AGE/EXPRESSION: ....

ORIGIN: .... **PRICE:** ....

SAMPLED: .... **RATING:** ☆☆☆☆☆

COLOR METER:

- MAHOGANY
- CARAMEL
- AMBER
- GOLD
- HONEY
- STRAW
- CLEAR

FLAVOR WHEEL:

HEAT/ABV: _____ %

BALANCE
FINISH
BODY
DARK FRUIT
ASTRIN-GENT
CITRUS FRUIT
SALTY
FLORAL
SWEET
SPICY
SMOKE
HERBAL/GRASSY
PEAT
MALT/CEREAL
TOFFEE

0.5
0.4
0.3
0.2
0.1

NOTES:
....
....
....
....
....
....

DISTILLER: . . . .

AGE/EXPRESSION: . . . .

ORIGIN: . . . .   PRICE: . . . .

SAMPLED: . . . .   RATING: ☆ ☆ ☆ ☆ ☆

COLOR METER:

- MAHOGANY
- CARAMEL
- AMBER
- GOLD
- HONEY
- STRAW
- CLEAR

FLAVOR WHEEL:

HEAT/ABV: . . . . %

BALANCE · FINISH · DARK FRUIT · CITRUS FRUIT · FLORAL · SPICY · HERBAL/GRASSY · MALT/CEREAL · TOFFEE · PEAT · SMOKE · SWEET · SALTY · ASTRINGENT · BODY

0.5 · 0.4 · 0.3 · 0.2 · 0.1

NOTES:

. . . .

. . . .

. . . .

. . . .

. . . .

DISTILLER: . . . .

AGE/EXPRESSION: . . . .

ORIGIN: . . . .   PRICE: . . . .

SAMPLED: . . . .   RATING: ☆ ☆ ☆ ☆ ☆

COLOR METER:

- MAHOGANY
- CARAMEL
- AMBER
- GOLD
- HONEY
- STRAW
- CLEAR

FLAVOR WHEEL:

HEAT/ABV: . . . . %

BALANCE   FINISH
BODY   DARK FRUIT
ASTRIN-GENT   CITRUS FRUIT
SALTY   FLORAL
SWEET   SPICY
SMOKE   HERBAL/GRASSY
PEAT   MALT/CEREAL
TOFFEE

0.5
0.4
0.3
0.2
0.1

NOTES:

. . . .

. . . .

. . . .

. . . .

. . . .

. . . .

👉 DISTILLER: . . . .

AGE/EXPRESSION: . . . .

ORIGIN: . . . .   PRICE: . . . .

SAMPLED: . . . .   RATING: ☆ ☆ ☆ ☆ ☆

COLOR METER:

- MAHOGANY
- CARAMEL
- AMBER
- GOLD
- HONEY
- STRAW
- CLEAR

FLAVOR WHEEL:

HEAT/ABV: . . . . %

BALANCE
FINISH
BODY
DARK FRUIT
ASTRIN-GENT
CITRUS FRUIT
SALTY
FLORAL
SWEET
SPICY
SMOKE
HERBAL/GRASSY
PEAT
TOFFEE
MALT/CEREAL

0.1 0.2 0.3 0.4 0.5

NOTES:

. . . .

. . . .

. . . .

. . . .

. . . .

. . . .

☞ **DISTILLER:** ....

AGE/EXPRESSION: ....

ORIGIN: .... **PRICE:** ....

SAMPLED: .... **RATING:** ☆ ☆ ☆ ☆ ☆

COLOR METER:

- MAHOGANY
- CARAMEL
- AMBER
- GOLD
- HONEY
- STRAW
- CLEAR

FLAVOR WHEEL:

HEAT/ABV: _____ %

BALANCE
FINISH
BODY
DARK FRUIT
ASTRIN-GENT
CITRUS FRUIT
SALTY
FLORAL
SWEET
SPICY
SMOKE
HERBAL/GRASSY
PEAT
MALT/CEREAL
TOFFEE

0.5 0.4 0.3 0.2 0.1

NOTES:

....
....
....
....
....

👉 **DISTILLER:** ....

AGE/EXPRESSION: ....

ORIGIN: .... **PRICE:** ....

SAMPLED: .... **RATING:** ☆ ☆ ☆ ☆ ☆

COLOR METER:

MAHOGANY

CARAMEL

AMBER

GOLD

HONEY

STRAW

CLEAR

FLAVOR WHEEL:

HEAT/
ABV: _____ %

BALANCE

FINISH

BODY

DARK FRUIT

ASTRIN-
GENT

CITRUS
FRUIT

SALTY

FLORAL

SWEET

SPICY

SMOKE

HERBAL/
GRASSY

PEAT

TOFFEE

MALT/
CEREAL

0.5
0.4
0.3
0.2
0.1

NOTES:

....

....

....

....

....

....

DISTILLER: ....

AGE/EXPRESSION: ....

ORIGIN: .... **PRICE:** ....

SAMPLED: .... **RATING:** ☆ ☆ ☆ ☆ ☆

COLOR METER:

- MAHOGANY
- CARAMEL
- AMBER
- GOLD
- HONEY
- STRAW
- CLEAR

FLAVOR WHEEL:

HEAT/ ABV: _____ %

BALANCE · FINISH · DARK FRUIT · BODY · CITRUS FRUIT · ASTRINGENT · FLORAL · SALTY · SPICY · SWEET · HERBAL/GRASSY · SMOKE · MALT/CEREAL · PEAT · TOFFEE

(scale: 0.1, 0.2, 0.3, 0.4, 0.5)

NOTES:

....

....

....

....

....

DISTILLER: ....

AGE/EXPRESSION: ....

ORIGIN: ....   **PRICE:** ....

SAMPLED: ....   **RATING:** ☆ ☆ ☆ ☆ ☆

COLOR METER:

- MAHOGANY
- CARAMEL
- AMBER
- GOLD
- HONEY
- STRAW
- CLEAR

FLAVOR WHEEL:

HEAT/ ABV: _____ %

BALANCE · FINISH · DARK FRUIT · CITRUS FRUIT · FLORAL · SPICY · HERBAL/GRASSY · MALT/CEREAL · TOFFEE · PEAT · SMOKE · SWEET · SALTY · ASTRINGENT · BODY

0.1 0.2 0.3 0.4 0.5

NOTES:

....

....

....

....

....

....

☞ **DISTILLER:** . . . .

AGE/EXPRESSION: . . . .

ORIGIN: . . . .   **PRICE:** . . . .

SAMPLED: . . . .   **RATING:** ☆ ☆ ☆ ☆ ☆

COLOR METER: **FLAVOR WHEEL:**

MAHOGANY

CARAMEL

AMBER

GOLD

HONEY

STRAW

CLEAR

BALANCE   FINISH

BODY   DARK FRUIT

HEAT/   %
ABV: . . . .

ASTRIN-   CITRUS
GENT   FRUIT

0.5
0.4
0.3
0.2
0.1

SALTY   FLORAL

SWEET   SPICY

                                               HERBAL/
SMOKE   GRASSY

                              MALT/
PEAT   TOFFEE   CEREAL

NOTES: . . . .

. . . .

. . . .

. . . .

. . . .

. . . .

👉 **DISTILLER:** . . . .

AGE/EXPRESSION: . . . .

ORIGIN: . . . . **PRICE:** . . . .

SAMPLED: . . . . **RATING:** ☆ ☆ ☆ ☆ ☆

COLOR METER:

- MAHOGANY
- CARAMEL
- AMBER
- GOLD
- HONEY
- STRAW
- CLEAR

FLAVOR WHEEL:

HEAT/ABV : _____ %

BALANCE · FINISH · BODY · DARK FRUIT · ASTRIN-GENT · CITRUS FRUIT · SALTY · FLORAL · SWEET · SPICY · SMOKE · HERBAL/GRASSY · PEAT · TOFFEE · MALT/CEREAL

0.5 0.4 0.3 0.2 0.1

NOTES: . . . .

. . . .

. . . .

. . . .

. . . .

. . . .

👉 **DISTILLER:** ....

AGE/EXPRESSION: ....

ORIGIN: .... **PRICE:** ....

SAMPLED: .... **RATING:** ☆ ☆ ☆ ☆ ☆

COLOR METER:

- MAHOGANY
- CARAMEL
- AMBER
- GOLD
- HONEY
- STRAW
- CLEAR

FLAVOR WHEEL:

HEAT/ABV: _____ %

BALANCE
FINISH
BODY
DARK FRUIT
ASTRIN-GENT
CITRUS FRUIT
SALTY
FLORAL
SWEET
SPICY
SMOKE
HERBAL/GRASSY
PEAT
TOFFEE
MALT/CEREAL

0.5
0.4
0.3
0.2
0.1

NOTES:

....
....
....
....
....
....

👉 **DISTILLER:** ....

AGE/EXPRESSION: ....

ORIGIN: .... **PRICE:** ....

SAMPLED: .... **RATING:** ☆ ☆ ☆ ☆ ☆

COLOR METER:

- MAHOGANY
- CARAMEL
- AMBER
- GOLD
- HONEY
- STRAW
- CLEAR

FLAVOR WHEEL:

HEAT/ABV : _____ %

FINISH
BALANCE
BODY
DARK FRUIT
ASTRIN-GENT
CITRUS FRUIT
SALTY
FLORAL
SWEET
SPICY
SMOKE
HERBAL/GRASSY
PEAT
TOFFEE
MALT/CEREAL

0.1 0.2 0.3 0.4 0.5

NOTES: ....
....
....
....
....
....

👉 **DISTILLER:** . . . .

AGE/EXPRESSION: . . . .

ORIGIN: . . . .   **PRICE:** . . . .

SAMPLED: . . . .   **RATING:** ☆ ☆ ☆ ☆ ☆

COLOR METER:

- MAHOGANY
- CARAMEL
- AMBER
- GOLD
- HONEY
- STRAW
- CLEAR

FLAVOR WHEEL:

BALANCE   FINISH

BODY

ASTRIN-GENT

SALTY

SWEET

SMOKE

PEAT   TOFFEE   MALT/CEREAL

DARK FRUIT

CITRUS FRUIT

FLORAL

SPICY

HERBAL/GRASSY

0.5 0.4 0.3 0.2 0.1

HEAT/ABV: _____ %

NOTES:

. . . .

. . . .

. . . .

. . . .

. . . .

DISTILLER: ....

AGE/EXPRESSION: ....

ORIGIN: .... PRICE: ....

SAMPLED: .... RATING: ☆ ☆ ☆ ☆ ☆

COLOR METER:

- MAHOGANY
- CARAMEL
- AMBER
- GOLD
- HONEY
- STRAW
- CLEAR

FLAVOR WHEEL:

HEAT/ ABV: _____ %

FINISH
BALANCE
BODY
ASTRIN-GENT
SALTY
SWEET
SMOKE
PEAT
TOFFEE
MALT/CEREAL
HERBAL/GRASSY
SPICY
FLORAL
CITRUS FRUIT
DARK FRUIT

0.5
0.4
0.3
0.2
0.1

NOTES:

....
....
....
....
....
....

☞ **DISTILLER:** ....

AGE/EXPRESSION: ....

ORIGIN: .... **PRICE:** ....

SAMPLED: .... **RATING:** ☆ ☆ ☆ ☆ ☆

COLOR METER:

MAHOGANY

CARAMEL

AMBER

GOLD

HONEY

STRAW

CLEAR

FLAVOR WHEEL:

HEAT/   %
ABV: _____

BALANCE   FINISH

BODY   DARK FRUIT

ASTRIN-GENT   CITRUS FRUIT

SALTY   FLORAL

SWEET   SPICY

SMOKE   HERBAL/GRASSY

PEAT   TOFFEE   MALT/CEREAL

0.1 0.2 0.3 0.4 0.5

NOTES: ....
....
....
....
....
....

👉 **DISTILLER:** . . . .

AGE/EXPRESSION: . . . .

ORIGIN: . . . . **PRICE:** . . . .

SAMPLED: . . . . **RATING:** ☆ ☆ ☆ ☆ ☆

COLOR METER:

- MAHOGANY
- CARAMEL
- AMBER
- GOLD
- HONEY
- STRAW
- CLEAR

FLAVOR WHEEL:

HEAT/
ABV : _____ %

BALANCE
BODY
FINISH
DARK FRUIT
ASTRIN-GENT
CITRUS FRUIT
SALTY
FLORAL
SWEET
SPICY
SMOKE
HERBAL/GRASSY
PEAT
TOFFEE
MALT/CEREAL

0.5
0.4
0.3
0.2
0.1

NOTES: . . . .

. . . .

. . . .

. . . .

. . . .

. . . .

👉 DISTILLER: ....

AGE/EXPRESSION: ....

ORIGIN: .... PRICE: ....

SAMPLED: .... RATING: ☆ ☆ ☆ ☆ ☆

COLOR METER:

- MAHOGANY
- CARAMEL
- AMBER
- GOLD
- HONEY
- STRAW
- CLEAR

FLAVOR WHEEL:

HEAT/ABV: _____ %

BALANCE
FINISH
BODY
DARK FRUIT
ASTRIN-GENT
CITRUS FRUIT
SALTY
FLORAL
SWEET
SPICY
SMOKE
HERBAL/GRASSY
PEAT
MALT/CEREAL
TOFFEE

0.5
0.4
0.3
0.2
0.1

NOTES:

....

....

....

....

....

....

DISTILLER: . . . .

AGE/EXPRESSION: . . . .

ORIGIN: . . . . PRICE: . . . .

SAMPLED: . . . . RATING: ☆ ☆ ☆ ☆ ☆

COLOR METER:

- MAHOGANY
- CARAMEL
- AMBER
- GOLD
- HONEY
- STRAW
- CLEAR

FLAVOR WHEEL:

HEAT/ABV: . . . . %

BALANCE
FINISH
BODY
DARK FRUIT
ASTRIN-GENT
CITRUS FRUIT
SALTY
FLORAL
SWEET
SPICY
SMOKE
HERBAL/GRASSY
PEAT
TOFFEE
MALT/CEREAL

0.5
0.4
0.3
0.2
0.1

NOTES:

. . . .

. . . .

. . . .

. . . .

. . . .

. . . .

DISTILLER: ....

AGE/EXPRESSION: ....

ORIGIN: .... **PRICE:** ....

SAMPLED: .... **RATING:** ☆ ☆ ☆ ☆ ☆

COLOR METER:

- MAHOGANY
- CARAMEL
- AMBER
- GOLD
- HONEY
- STRAW
- CLEAR

FLAVOR WHEEL:

HEAT/ABV: _____ %

BALANCE
FINISH
BODY
DARK FRUIT
ASTRIN-GENT
CITRUS FRUIT
SALTY
FLORAL
SWEET
SPICY
SMOKE
HERBAL/GRASSY
PEAT
TOFFEE
MALT/CEREAL

0.5 0.4 0.3 0.2 0.1

NOTES:

....

....

....

....

....

....

☞ **DISTILLER:** . . . .

AGE/EXPRESSION: . . . .

ORIGIN: . . . . **PRICE:** . . . .

SAMPLED: . . . . **RATING:** ☆ ☆ ☆ ☆ ☆

COLOR METER:

- MAHOGANY
- CARAMEL
- AMBER
- GOLD
- HONEY
- STRAW
- CLEAR

FLAVOR WHEEL:

HEAT/ABV: . . . . %

FINISH
BALANCE
BODY
DARK FRUIT
ASTRIN-GENT
CITRUS FRUIT
SALTY
FLORAL
SWEET
SPICY
SMOKE
HERBAL/GRASSY
PEAT
TOFFEE
MALT/CEREAL

0.5 0.4 0.3 0.2 0.1

NOTES: . . . .

. . . .

. . . .

. . . .

. . . .

. . . .

☞ **DISTILLER:** ....

AGE/EXPRESSION: ....

ORIGIN: .... **PRICE:** ....

SAMPLED: .... **RATING:** ☆ ☆ ☆ ☆ ☆

COLOR METER:

- MAHOGANY
- CARAMEL
- AMBER
- GOLD
- HONEY
- STRAW
- CLEAR

FLAVOR WHEEL:

HEAT/ ABV: _____ %

BALANCE

FINISH

BODY

DARK FRUIT

ASTRIN-GENT

CITRUS FRUIT

SALTY

FLORAL

SWEET

SPICY

SMOKE

HERBAL/ GRASSY

PEAT

MALT/ CEREAL

TOFFEE

#5 #4 #3 #2 #1

NOTES: ....
....
....
....
....
....

☞ DISTILLER: . . . .

AGE/EXPRESSION: . . . .

ORIGIN: . . . .   PRICE: . . . .

SAMPLED: . . . .   RATING: ☆ ☆ ☆ ☆ ☆

COLOR METER:

- MAHOGANY
- CARAMEL
- AMBER
- GOLD
- HONEY
- STRAW
- CLEAR

FLAVOR WHEEL:

HEAT/ABV: . . . . %

FINISH
BALANCE
BODY
DARK FRUIT
ASTRIN-GENT
CITRUS FRUIT
SALTY
FLORAL
SWEET
SPICY
SMOKE
HERBAL/GRASSY
PEAT
TOFFEE
MALT/CEREAL

0.5
0.4
0.3
0.2
0.1

NOTES:

. . . .

. . . .

. . . .

. . . .

. . . .

. . . .

DISTILLER: . . . .

AGE/EXPRESSION: . . . .

ORIGIN: . . . . **PRICE:** . . . .

SAMPLED: . . . . **RATING:** ☆ ☆ ☆ ☆ ☆

COLOR METER:

- MAHOGANY
- CARAMEL
- AMBER
- GOLD
- HONEY
- STRAW
- CLEAR

FLAVOR WHEEL:

HEAT/   %
ABV: _____

BALANCE   FINISH

BODY   DARK FRUIT

ASTRIN-   CITRUS
GENT   FRUIT

SALTY   FLORAL

SWEET   SPICY

SMOKE   HERBAL/
GRASSY

PEAT   TOFFEE   MALT/
CEREAL

(wheel rings labeled: 01, 02, 03, 04, 05)

NOTES:

. . . .

. . . .

. . . .

. . . .

. . . .

. . . .

👉 **DISTILLER:** ....

AGE/EXPRESSION: ....

ORIGIN: .... **PRICE:** ....

SAMPLED: .... **RATING:** ☆ ☆ ☆ ☆ ☆

COLOR METER:

- MAHOGANY
- CARAMEL
- AMBER
- GOLD
- HONEY
- STRAW
- CLEAR

FLAVOR WHEEL:

HEAT/ABV: _____ %

BALANCE
FINISH
BODY
DARK FRUIT
ASTRIN-GENT
CITRUS FRUIT
SALTY
FLORAL
SWEET
SPICY
SMOKE
HERBAL/GRASSY
PEAT
MALT/CEREAL
TOFFEE

0.1 0.2 0.3 0.4 0.5

NOTES: ....
....
....
....
....
....

☞ **DISTILLER:** ....

AGE/EXPRESSION: ....

ORIGIN: .... **PRICE:** ....

SAMPLED: .... **RATING:** ☆ ☆ ☆ ☆ ☆

COLOR METER: **FLAVOR WHEEL:**

MAHOGANY

CARAMEL

AMBER

GOLD

HONEY

STRAW

CLEAR

HEAT/ABV: _____ %

BALANCE   FINISH

BODY   DARK FRUIT

ASTRIN-GENT   CITRUS FRUIT

SALTY   FLORAL

SWEET   SPICY

SMOKE   HERBAL/GRASSY

PEAT   TOFFEE   MALT/CEREAL

0.5 0.4 0.3 0.2 0.1

NOTES: ....
....
....
....
....
....

👉 **DISTILLER:** ....

AGE/EXPRESSION: ....

ORIGIN: .... **PRICE:** ....

SAMPLED: .... **RATING:** ☆☆☆☆☆

COLOR METER:

- MAHOGANY
- CARAMEL
- AMBER
- GOLD
- HONEY
- STRAW
- CLEAR

FLAVOR WHEEL:

HEAT/ABV: _____ %

FINISH
BALANCE
BODY
DARK FRUIT
ASTRIN-GENT
CITRUS FRUIT
SALTY
FLORAL
SWEET
SPICY
SMOKE
HERBAL/GRASSY
PEAT
TOFFEE
MALT/CEREAL

0.1 0.2 0.3 0.4 0.5

NOTES:
....
....
....
....
....

DISTILLER: ....

AGE/EXPRESSION: ....

ORIGIN: .... PRICE: ....

SAMPLED: .... RATING: ☆ ☆ ☆ ☆ ☆

COLOR METER:

- MAHOGANY
- CARAMEL
- AMBER
- GOLD
- HONEY
- STRAW
- CLEAR

FLAVOR WHEEL:

HEAT/
ABV: _____ %

BALANCE
FINISH
BODY
DARK FRUIT
ASTRIN-
GENT
CITRUS
FRUIT
SALTY
0.5
0.4
0.3
0.2
0.1
FLORAL
SWEET
SPICY
SMOKE
HERBAL/
GRASSY
PEAT
MALT/
CEREAL
TOFFEE

NOTES:

....
....
....
....
....

DISTILLER: ....

AGE/EXPRESSION: ....

ORIGIN: .... **PRICE:** ....

SAMPLED: .... **RATING:** ☆ ☆ ☆ ☆ ☆

COLOR METER:

- MAHOGANY
- CARAMEL
- AMBER
- GOLD
- HONEY
- STRAW
- CLEAR

FLAVOR WHEEL:

HEAT/ABV: _____ %

FINISH
BALANCE
BODY
DARK FRUIT
ASTRIN-GENT
CITRUS FRUIT
SALTY
FLORAL
SWEET
SPICY
SMOKE
HERBAL/GRASSY
PEAT
TOFFEE
MALT/CEREAL

0.5 0.4 0.3 0.2 0.1

NOTES: ....

....

....

....

....

....

DISTILLER: ....

AGE/EXPRESSION: ....

ORIGIN: .... PRICE: ....

SAMPLED: .... RATING: ☆ ☆ ☆ ☆ ☆

COLOR METER:

- MAHOGANY
- CARAMEL
- AMBER
- GOLD
- HONEY
- STRAW
- CLEAR

FLAVOR WHEEL:

HEAT/ ABV: _____ %

BALANCE

FINISH

BODY

DARK FRUIT

ASTRIN-GENT

CITRUS FRUIT

SALTY

FLORAL

SWEET

SPICY

SMOKE

HERBAL/ GRASSY

PEAT

TOFFEE

MALT/ CEREAL

0.5
0.4
0.3
0.2
0.1

NOTES:

....
....
....
....
....
....

👉 **DISTILLER:** ....

AGE/EXPRESSION: ....

ORIGIN: .... **PRICE:** ....

SAMPLED: .... **RATING:** ☆☆☆☆☆

COLOR METER: FLAVOR WHEEL:

COLOR METER:
- MAHOGANY
- CARAMEL
- AMBER
- GOLD
- HONEY
- STRAW
- CLEAR

FLAVOR WHEEL:

HEAT/ ABV: _____ %

BALANCE — FINISH
BODY — DARK FRUIT
ASTRIN-GENT — CITRUS FRUIT
SALTY — FLORAL
SWEET — SPICY
SMOKE — HERBAL/GRASSY
PEAT — MALT/CEREAL
TOFFEE

0.5 0.4 0.3 0.2 0.1

NOTES: ....

....

....

....

....

....

DISTILLER: . . . .

AGE/EXPRESSION: . . . .

ORIGIN: . . . . PRICE: . . . .

SAMPLED: . . . . RATING: ☆ ☆ ☆ ☆ ☆

COLOR METER:

MAHOGANY

CARAMEL

AMBER

GOLD

HONEY

STRAW

CLEAR

FLAVOR WHEEL:

BALANCE   FINISH

BODY

ASTRIN-GENT

SALTY

SWEET

SMOKE

PEAT   TOFFEE

DARK FRUIT

CITRUS FRUIT

FLORAL

SPICY

HERBAL/GRASSY

MALT/CEREAL

HEAT/ABV: _____ %

0.5
0.4
0.3
0.2
0.1

NOTES:

. . . .

. . . .

. . . .

. . . .

. . . .

👉 **DISTILLER:** ....

AGE/EXPRESSION: ....

ORIGIN: .... **PRICE:** ....

SAMPLED: .... **RATING:** ☆ ☆ ☆ ☆ ☆

COLOR METER: FLAVOR WHEEL:

COLOR METER:

- MAHOGANY
- CARAMEL
- AMBER
- GOLD
- HONEY
- STRAW
- CLEAR

FLAVOR WHEEL:

HEAT/ABV: _____ %

BALANCE
FINISH
BODY
DARK FRUIT
ASTRIN-GENT
CITRUS FRUIT
SALTY
FLORAL
SWEET
SPICY
SMOKE
HERBAL/GRASSY
PEAT
TOFFEE
MALT/CEREAL

0.5
0.4
0.3
0.2
0.1

NOTES:

....

....

....

....

....

....

👉 **DISTILLER:** ....

AGE/EXPRESSION: ....

ORIGIN: .... **PRICE:** ....

SAMPLED: .... **RATING:** ☆ ☆ ☆ ☆ ☆

COLOR METER: **FLAVOR WHEEL:**

MAHOGANY

CARAMEL

AMBER

GOLD

HONEY

STRAW

CLEAR

BALANCE   FINISH

BODY

ASTRIN-GENT

SALTY

SWEET

SMOKE

PEAT

TOFFEE

MALT/CEREAL

HERBAL/GRASSY

SPICY

FLORAL

CITRUS FRUIT

DARK FRUIT

0.5
0.4
0.3
0.2
0.1

HEAT/ABV: _____ %

NOTES: ....
....
....
....
....
....

👉 **DISTILLER:** . . . .

AGE/EXPRESSION: . . . .

ORIGIN: . . . .   **PRICE:** . . . .

SAMPLED: . . . .   **RATING:** ☆ ☆ ☆ ☆ ☆

COLOR METER:

- MAHOGANY
- CARAMEL
- AMBER
- GOLD
- HONEY
- STRAW
- CLEAR

FLAVOR WHEEL:

HEAT/ABV: _____ %

FINISH
BALANCE
BODY
DARK FRUIT
ASTRIN-GENT
CITRUS FRUIT
SALTY
FLORAL
SWEET
SPICY
SMOKE
HERBAL/GRASSY
PEAT
TOFFEE
MALT/CEREAL

0.1 0.2 0.3 0.4 0.5

NOTES:

. . . .

. . . .

. . . .

. . . .

. . . .

. . . .

👉 **DISTILLER:** ....

AGE/EXPRESSION: ....

ORIGIN: .... **PRICE:** ....

SAMPLED: .... **RATING:** ☆ ☆ ☆ ☆ ☆

COLOR METER:

- MAHOGANY
- CARAMEL
- AMBER
- GOLD
- HONEY
- STRAW
- CLEAR

FLAVOR WHEEL:

HEAT/ ABV: _____ %

BALANCE · FINISH · DARK FRUIT · CITRUS FRUIT · FLORAL · SPICY · HERBAL/ GRASSY · MALT/ CEREAL · TOFFEE · PEAT · SMOKE · SWEET · SALTY · ASTRIN-GENT · BODY

0.5
0.4
0.3
0.2
0.1

NOTES:

....
....
....
....
....

☞ **DISTILLER:** . . . .

AGE/EXPRESSION: . . . .

ORIGIN: . . . . **PRICE:** . . . .

SAMPLED: . . . . **RATING:** ☆ ☆ ☆ ☆ ☆

COLOR METER:

- MAHOGANY
- CARAMEL
- AMBER
- GOLD
- HONEY
- STRAW
- CLEAR

FLAVOR WHEEL:

HEAT/ABV : _____ %

BALANCE
FINISH
BODY
DARK FRUIT
ASTRIN-GENT
CITRUS FRUIT
SALTY
FLORAL
SWEET
SPICY
SMOKE
HERBAL/GRASSY
PEAT
TOFFEE
MALT/CEREAL

0.5 0.4 0.3 0.2 0.1

NOTES:

. . . .

. . . .

. . . .

. . . .

. . . .

👉 **DISTILLER:** . . . .

AGE/EXPRESSION: . . . .

ORIGIN: . . . .   **PRICE:** . . . .

SAMPLED: . . . .   **RATING:** ☆ ☆ ☆ ☆ ☆

COLOR METER:

- MAHOGANY
- CARAMEL
- AMBER
- GOLD
- HONEY
- STRAW
- CLEAR

FLAVOR WHEEL:

HEAT/   %
ABV : _____

BALANCE   FINISH

BODY   DARK FRUIT

ASTRIN-GENT   CITRUS FRUIT

SALTY   FLORAL

SWEET   SPICY

SMOKE   HERBAL/ GRASSY

PEAT   TOFFEE   MALT/ CEREAL

0.5   0.4   0.3   0.2   0.1

NOTES:

. . . .

. . . .

. . . .

. . . .

. . . .

👉 **DISTILLER:** ....

AGE/EXPRESSION: ....

ORIGIN: .... **PRICE:** ....

SAMPLED: .... **RATING:** ☆☆☆☆☆

COLOR METER:

- MAHOGANY
- CARAMEL
- AMBER
- GOLD
- HONEY
- STRAW
- CLEAR

FLAVOR WHEEL:

HEAT/ABV : _____ %

FINISH

BALANCE

BODY

DARK FRUIT

ASTRIN-GENT

CITRUS FRUIT

SALTY

FLORAL

SWEET

SPICY

SMOKE

HERBAL/GRASSY

PEAT

TOFFEE

MALT/CEREAL

0.1 0.2 0.3 0.4 0.5

NOTES: ....
....
....
....
....
....

DISTILLER: ....

AGE/EXPRESSION: ....

ORIGIN: .... **PRICE:** ....

SAMPLED: .... **RATING:** ☆ ☆ ☆ ☆ ☆

COLOR METER:

- MAHOGANY
- CARAMEL
- AMBER
- GOLD
- HONEY
- STRAW
- CLEAR

FLAVOR WHEEL:

HEAT/ ABV: _____ %

BALANCE
FINISH
BODY
DARK FRUIT
ASTRIN-GENT
CITRUS FRUIT
SALTY
FLORAL
SWEET
SPICY
SMOKE
HERBAL/ GRASSY
PEAT
TOFFEE
MALT/ CEREAL

0.5 0.4 0.3 0.2 0.1

NOTES:

....
....
....
....
....
....

👉 **DISTILLER:** ....

AGE/EXPRESSION: ....

ORIGIN: .... **PRICE:** ....

SAMPLED: .... **RATING:** ☆ ☆ ☆ ☆ ☆

COLOR METER:

- MAHOGANY
- CARAMEL
- AMBER
- GOLD
- HONEY
- STRAW
- CLEAR

FLAVOR WHEEL:

HEAT/ABV: _____ %

BALANCE
FINISH
BODY
DARK FRUIT
ASTRIN-GENT
CITRUS FRUIT
SALTY
FLORAL
SWEET
SPICY
SMOKE
HERBAL/GRASSY
PEAT
TOFFEE
MALT/CEREAL

0.1 0.2 0.3 0.4 0.5

NOTES:

....
....
....
....
....
....

DISTILLER: ....

AGE/EXPRESSION: ....

ORIGIN: .... **PRICE:** ....

SAMPLED: .... **RATING:** ☆☆☆☆☆

COLOR METER:

- MAHOGANY
- CARAMEL
- AMBER
- GOLD
- HONEY
- STRAW
- CLEAR

FLAVOR WHEEL:

HEAT/   %
ABV: _____

BALANCE   FINISH

BODY

ASTRIN-GENT

SALTY

SWEET

SMOKE

PEAT   TOFFEE   MALT/CEREAL

DARK FRUIT

CITRUS FRUIT

FLORAL

SPICY

HERBAL/GRASSY

0.5
0.4
0.3
0.2
0.1

NOTES:

....
....
....
....
....

👉 **DISTILLER:** ....

AGE/EXPRESSION: ....

ORIGIN: .... **PRICE:** ....

SAMPLED: .... **RATING:** ☆☆☆☆☆

COLOR METER:

- MAHOGANY
- CARAMEL
- AMBER
- GOLD
- HONEY
- STRAW
- CLEAR

FLAVOR WHEEL:

HEAT/ABV : _____ %

BALANCE
FINISH
BODY
DARK FRUIT
ASTRIN-GENT
CITRUS FRUIT
SALTY
FLORAL
SWEET
SPICY
SMOKE
HERBAL/GRASSY
PEAT
TOFFEE
MALT/CEREAL

0.5
0.4
0.3
0.2
0.1

NOTES:

....
....
....
....
....

☛ DISTILLER: ....

AGE/EXPRESSION: ....

ORIGIN: .... PRICE: ....

SAMPLED: .... RATING: ☆☆☆☆☆

COLOR METER:

- MAHOGANY
- CARAMEL
- AMBER
- GOLD
- HONEY
- STRAW
- CLEAR

FLAVOR WHEEL:

HEAT/ ABV: _____ %

BALANCE
FINISH
BODY
DARK FRUIT
ASTRIN-GENT
CITRUS FRUIT
SALTY
FLORAL
SWEET
SPICY
SMOKE
HERBAL/ GRASSY
PEAT
TOFFEE
MALT/ CEREAL

0.5
0.4
0.3
0.2
0.1

NOTES:

....
....
....
....
....

👉 **DISTILLER:** ....

AGE/EXPRESSION: ....

ORIGIN: .... **PRICE:** ....

SAMPLED: .... **RATING:** ☆ ☆ ☆ ☆ ☆

COLOR METER:

- MAHOGANY
- CARAMEL
- AMBER
- GOLD
- HONEY
- STRAW
- CLEAR

FLAVOR WHEEL:

HEAT/ABV: _____ %

BALANCE
FINISH
BODY
DARK FRUIT
ASTRIN-GENT
CITRUS FRUIT
SALTY
FLORAL
SWEET
SPICY
SMOKE
HERBAL/GRASSY
PEAT
TOFFEE
MALT/CEREAL

0.5 0.4 0.3 0.2 0.1

NOTES:

....

....

....

....

....

👉 **DISTILLER:** ....

AGE/EXPRESSION: ....

ORIGIN: .... **PRICE:** ....

SAMPLED: .... **RATING:** ☆☆☆☆☆

COLOR METER:

- MAHOGANY
- CARAMEL
- AMBER
- GOLD
- HONEY
- STRAW
- CLEAR

FLAVOR WHEEL:

HEAT/ABV: _____ %

BALANCE
FINISH
BODY
DARK FRUIT
ASTRIN-GENT
CITRUS FRUIT
SALTY
FLORAL
SWEET
SPICY
SMOKE
HERBAL/GRASSY
PEAT
MALT/CEREAL
TOFFEE

0.5
0.4
0.3
0.2
0.1

NOTES:

....

....

....

....

....

....

☞ DISTILLER: ....

AGE/EXPRESSION: ....

ORIGIN: .... PRICE: ....

SAMPLED: .... RATING: ☆☆☆☆☆

COLOR METER:

- MAHOGANY
- CARAMEL
- AMBER
- GOLD
- HONEY
- STRAW
- CLEAR

FLAVOR WHEEL:

HEAT/ABV: _____ %

Wheel labels: FINISH, DARK FRUIT, CITRUS FRUIT, FLORAL, SPICY, HERBAL/GRASSY, MALT/CEREAL, TOFFEE, PEAT, SMOKE, SWEET, SALTY, ASTRINGENT, BODY, BALANCE

Scale: 0.1, 0.2, 0.3, 0.4, 0.5

NOTES:

....
....
....
....
....
....

👉 **DISTILLER:** ....

AGE/EXPRESSION: ....

ORIGIN: .... **PRICE:** ....

SAMPLED: .... **RATING:** ☆☆☆☆☆

COLOR METER:

- MAHOGANY
- CARAMEL
- AMBER
- GOLD
- HONEY
- STRAW
- CLEAR

FLAVOR WHEEL:

HEAT/ _____ %
ABV: _____

BALANCE · FINISH
BODY
ASTRIN-GENT
SALTY
SWEET
SMOKE
PEAT
TOFFEE
MALT/CEREAL
HERBAL/GRASSY
SPICY
FLORAL
CITRUS FRUIT
DARK FRUIT

5 4 3 2 1

NOTES:
....
....
....
....
....
....

DISTILLER: ....

AGE/EXPRESSION: ....

ORIGIN: .... **PRICE:** ....

SAMPLED: .... **RATING:** ☆☆☆☆☆

COLOR METER:

- MAHOGANY
- CARAMEL
- AMBER
- GOLD
- HONEY
- STRAW
- CLEAR

FLAVOR WHEEL:

HEAT/ABV: _____ %

FINISH
BALANCE
BODY
DARK FRUIT
ASTRIN-GENT
CITRUS FRUIT
SALTY
FLORAL
SWEET
SPICY
SMOKE
HERBAL/GRASSY
PEAT
TOFFEE
MALT/CEREAL

0.1 0.2 0.3 0.4 0.5

NOTES:

....
....
....
....
....
....

DISTILLER: ....

AGE/EXPRESSION: ....

ORIGIN: .... **PRICE:** ....

SAMPLED: .... **RATING:** ☆ ☆ ☆ ☆ ☆

COLOR METER:

- MAHOGANY
- CARAMEL
- AMBER
- GOLD
- HONEY
- STRAW
- CLEAR

FLAVOR WHEEL:

HEAT / ABV: _____ %

BALANCE
FINISH
BODY
DARK FRUIT
ASTRIN-GENT
CITRUS FRUIT
SALTY
FLORAL
SWEET
SPICY
SMOKE
HERBAL/ GRASSY
PEAT
MALT/ CEREAL
TOFFEE

0.1 0.2 0.3 0.4 0.5

NOTES:

....

....

....

....

....

....

👉 **DISTILLER:** ....

AGE/EXPRESSION: ....

ORIGIN: .... **PRICE:** ....

SAMPLED: .... **RATING:** ☆☆☆☆☆

COLOR METER:

- MAHOGANY
- CARAMEL
- AMBER
- GOLD
- HONEY
- STRAW
- CLEAR

FLAVOR WHEEL:

HEAT/ABV: _____ %

FINISH
BALANCE
BODY
DARK FRUIT
ASTRIN-GENT
CITRUS FRUIT
SALTY
FLORAL
SWEET
SPICY
SMOKE
HERBAL/GRASSY
PEAT
TOFFEE
MALT/CEREAL

05
04
03
02
01

NOTES:

....

....

....

....

....

....

DISTILLER: ....

AGE/EXPRESSION: ....

ORIGIN: .... PRICE: ....

SAMPLED: .... RATING: ☆ ☆ ☆ ☆ ☆

COLOR METER:

- MAHOGANY
- CARAMEL
- AMBER
- GOLD
- HONEY
- STRAW
- CLEAR

FLAVOR WHEEL:

HEAT/ _____ %
ABV: _____

BALANCE
FINISH
BODY
DARK FRUIT
ASTRIN-GENT
CITRUS FRUIT
SALTY
FLORAL
SWEET
SPICY
SMOKE
HERBAL/ GRASSY
PEAT
MALT/ CEREAL
TOFFEE

05
04
03
02
01

NOTES:

....
....
....
....
....

DISTILLER: ....

AGE/EXPRESSION: ....

ORIGIN: .... **PRICE:** ....

SAMPLED: .... **RATING:** ☆ ☆ ☆ ☆ ☆

COLOR METER:

- MAHOGANY
- CARAMEL
- AMBER
- GOLD
- HONEY
- STRAW
- CLEAR

FLAVOR WHEEL:

HEAT/ABV : _____ %

BALANCE
FINISH
BODY
DARK FRUIT
ASTRIN-GENT
CITRUS FRUIT
SALTY
FLORAL
SWEET
SPICY
SMOKE
HERBAL/GRASSY
PEAT
TOFFEE
MALT/CEREAL

0.1 0.2 0.3 0.4 0.5

NOTES:

....
....
....
....
....

👉 DISTILLER: . . . .

AGE/EXPRESSION: . . . .

ORIGIN: . . . . PRICE: . . . .

SAMPLED: . . . . RATING: ☆☆☆☆☆

COLOR METER:

- MAHOGANY
- CARAMEL
- AMBER
- GOLD
- HONEY
- STRAW
- CLEAR

FLAVOR WHEEL:

HEAT/ABV: . . . . %

BALANCE FINISH

BODY DARK FRUIT

ASTRIN-GENT CITRUS FRUIT

SALTY FLORAL

SWEET SPICY

SMOKE HERBAL/GRASSY

PEAT TOFFEE MALT/CEREAL

0.1 0.2 0.3 0.4 0.5

NOTES:

. . . .

. . . .

. . . .

. . . .

. . . .

DISTILLER: ....

AGE/EXPRESSION: ....

ORIGIN: .... **PRICE:** ....

SAMPLED: .... **RATING:** ☆☆☆☆☆

COLOR METER:

- MAHOGANY
- CARAMEL
- AMBER
- GOLD
- HONEY
- STRAW
- CLEAR

FLAVOR WHEEL:

HEAT/ABV: _____ %

FINISH
BALANCE
BODY
DARK FRUIT
ASTRIN-GENT
CITRUS FRUIT
SALTY
FLORAL
SWEET
SPICY
SMOKE
HERBAL/GRASSY
PEAT
TOFFEE
MALT/CEREAL

0.1 0.2 0.3 0.4 0.5

NOTES:

....
....
....
....
....
....

👉 **DISTILLER:** ....

AGE/EXPRESSION: ....

ORIGIN: .... **PRICE:** ....

SAMPLED: .... **RATING:** ☆ ☆ ☆ ☆ ☆

COLOR METER: FLAVOR WHEEL:

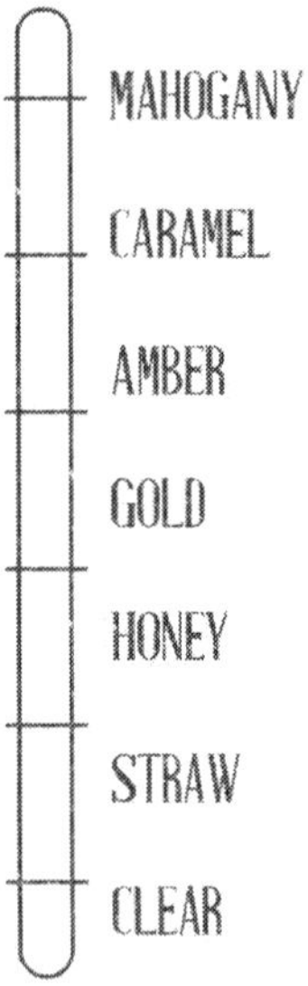

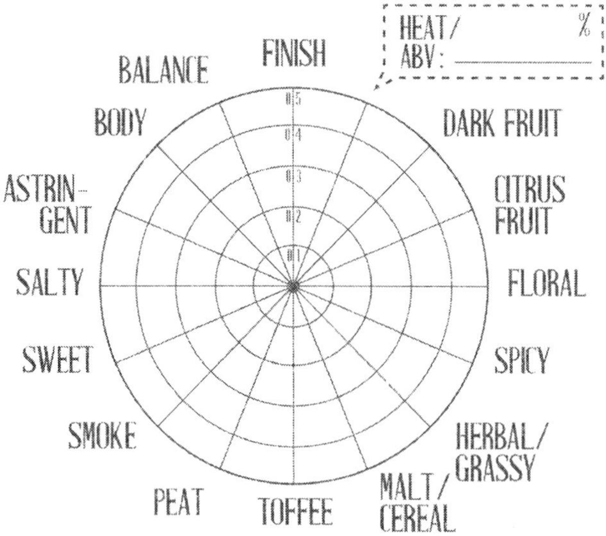

COLOR METER scale (top to bottom):
- MAHOGANY
- CARAMEL
- AMBER
- GOLD
- HONEY
- STRAW
- CLEAR

FLAVOR WHEEL labels:
- FINISH
- BALANCE
- BODY
- DARK FRUIT
- ASTRIN-GENT
- CITRUS FRUIT
- SALTY
- FLORAL
- SWEET
- SPICY
- SMOKE
- HERBAL/GRASSY
- PEAT
- TOFFEE
- MALT/CEREAL

Wheel scale: 0.1, 0.2, 0.3, 0.4, 0.5

HEAT/ABV: _____ %

NOTES:
....
....
....
....
....

👉 **DISTILLER:** . . . .

AGE/EXPRESSION: . . . .

ORIGIN: . . . . **PRICE:** . . . .

SAMPLED: . . . . **RATING:** ☆ ☆ ☆ ☆ ☆

COLOR METER:

- MAHOGANY
- CARAMEL
- AMBER
- GOLD
- HONEY
- STRAW
- CLEAR

FLAVOR WHEEL:

HEAT/ABV: _____ %

FINISH
BALANCE
BODY
DARK FRUIT
ASTRIN-GENT
CITRUS FRUIT
SALTY
FLORAL
SWEET
SPICY
SMOKE
HERBAL/GRASSY
PEAT
TOFFEE
MALT/CEREAL

0.5
0.4
0.3
0.2
0.1

NOTES:

. . . .
. . . .
. . . .
. . . .
. . . .
. . . .

👉 **DISTILLER:** ....

AGE/EXPRESSION: ....

ORIGIN: .... **PRICE:** ....

SAMPLED: .... **RATING:** ☆☆☆☆☆

COLOR METER:

- MAHOGANY
- CARAMEL
- AMBER
- GOLD
- HONEY
- STRAW
- CLEAR

FLAVOR WHEEL:

HEAT/ ABV: _____ %

BALANCE — FINISH — DARK FRUIT — CITRUS FRUIT — FLORAL — SPICY — HERBAL/ GRASSY — MALT/ CEREAL — TOFFEE — PEAT — SMOKE — SWEET — SALTY — ASTRIN-GENT — BODY

#5 #4 #3 #2 #1

NOTES:

....
....
....
....
....
....

👉 **DISTILLER:** ....

AGE/EXPRESSION: ....

ORIGIN: ....   **PRICE:** ....

SAMPLED: ....   **RATING:** ☆ ☆ ☆ ☆ ☆

COLOR METER:

- MAHOGANY
- CARAMEL
- AMBER
- GOLD
- HONEY
- STRAW
- CLEAR

FLAVOR WHEEL:

HEAT/ABV: _____ %

BALANCE
FINISH
BODY
DARK FRUIT
ASTRIN-GENT
CITRUS FRUIT
SALTY
FLORAL
SWEET
SPICY
SMOKE
HERBAL/GRASSY
PEAT
TOFFEE
MALT/CEREAL

0.5
0.4
0.3
0.2
0.1

NOTES:

....
....
....
....
....
....

☞ **DISTILLER:** ....

AGE/EXPRESSION: ....

ORIGIN: .... **PRICE:** ....

SAMPLED: .... **RATING:** ☆ ☆ ☆ ☆ ☆

COLOR METER:

- MAHOGANY
- CARAMEL
- AMBER
- GOLD
- HONEY
- STRAW
- CLEAR

FLAVOR WHEEL:

HEAT/ _____ %
ABV: _____

BALANCE
BODY
FINISH
ASTRIN-GENT
DARK FRUIT
SALTY
CITRUS FRUIT
SWEET
FLORAL
SMOKE
SPICY
PEAT
HERBAL/ GRASSY
TOFFEE
MALT/ CEREAL

NOTES: ....

....

....

....

....

....

👉 **DISTILLER:** ....

AGE/EXPRESSION: ....

ORIGIN: .... **PRICE:** ....

SAMPLED: .... **RATING:** ☆ ☆ ☆ ☆ ☆

COLOR METER:

- MAHOGANY
- CARAMEL
- AMBER
- GOLD
- HONEY
- STRAW
- CLEAR

FLAVOR WHEEL:

HEAT/ABV: _____ %

BALANCE, FINISH, BODY, DARK FRUIT, ASTRIN-GENT, CITRUS FRUIT, SALTY, FLORAL, SWEET, SPICY, SMOKE, HERBAL/GRASSY, PEAT, TOFFEE, MALT/CEREAL

0.1 0.2 0.3 0.4 0.5

NOTES: ....

....

....

....

....

....

DISTILLER: ....

AGE/EXPRESSION: ....

ORIGIN: .... **PRICE:** ....

SAMPLED: .... **RATING:** ☆ ☆ ☆ ☆ ☆

COLOR METER:

- MAHOGANY
- CARAMEL
- AMBER
- GOLD
- HONEY
- STRAW
- CLEAR

FLAVOR WHEEL:

HEAT/ %
ABV: _____

BALANCE
FINISH
BODY
DARK FRUIT
ASTRIN-GENT
CITRUS FRUIT
SALTY
FLORAL
SWEET
SPICY
SMOKE
HERBAL/GRASSY
PEAT
TOFFEE
MALT/CEREAL

0.5
0.4
0.3
0.2
0.1

NOTES:

....
....
....
....
....

👉 DISTILLER: . . . .

AGE/EXPRESSION: . . . .

ORIGIN: . . . . PRICE: . . . .

SAMPLED: . . . . RATING: ☆ ☆ ☆ ☆ ☆

COLOR METER:

MAHOGANY

CARAMEL

AMBER

GOLD

HONEY

STRAW

CLEAR

FLAVOR WHEEL:

HEAT/ %
ABV: . . . .

FINISH

BALANCE

BODY

DARK FRUIT

ASTRIN-
GENT

CITRUS
FRUIT

SALTY

FLORAL

SWEET

SPICY

SMOKE

HERBAL/
GRASSY

PEAT

TOFFEE

MALT/
CEREAL

0.5
0.4
0.3
0.2
0.1

NOTES:

. . . .

. . . .

. . . .

. . . .

. . . .

. . . .

☞ **DISTILLER:** . . . .

AGE/EXPRESSION: . . . .

ORIGIN: . . . .   **PRICE:** . . . .

SAMPLED: . . . .   **RATING:** ☆ ☆ ☆ ☆ ☆

COLOR METER:

- MAHOGANY
- CARAMEL
- AMBER
- GOLD
- HONEY
- STRAW
- CLEAR

FLAVOR WHEEL:

HEAT/ABV: _____ %

BALANCE • FINISH • DARK FRUIT • CITRUS FRUIT • FLORAL • SPICY • HERBAL/GRASSY • MALT/CEREAL • TOFFEE • PEAT • SMOKE • SWEET • SALTY • ASTRIN-GENT • BODY

0.1 0.2 0.3 0.4 0.5

NOTES:

. . . .

. . . .

. . . .

. . . .

. . . .

DISTILLER: ....

AGE/EXPRESSION: ....

ORIGIN: ....   PRICE: ....

SAMPLED: ....   RATING: ☆ ☆ ☆ ☆ ☆

COLOR METER:

- MAHOGANY
- CARAMEL
- AMBER
- GOLD
- HONEY
- STRAW
- CLEAR

FLAVOR WHEEL:

HEAT/ABV: .... %

BALANCE

FINISH

BODY

DARK FRUIT

ASTRIN-GENT

CITRUS FRUIT

SALTY

FLORAL

SWEET

SPICY

SMOKE

HERBAL/GRASSY

PEAT

TOFFEE

MALT/CEREAL

0.5
0.4
0.3
0.2
0.1

NOTES:

....
....
....
....
....
....

☞ **DISTILLER:** . . . .

AGE/EXPRESSION: . . . .

ORIGIN: . . . . **PRICE:** . . . .

SAMPLED: . . . . **RATING:** ☆ ☆ ☆ ☆ ☆

COLOR METER:

- MAHOGANY
- CARAMEL
- AMBER
- GOLD
- HONEY
- STRAW
- CLEAR

FLAVOR WHEEL:

HEAT/ %
ABV: _____

BALANCE   FINISH
BODY

ASTRIN-GENT   DARK FRUIT

SALTY   0.5   CITRUS FRUIT
              0.4
              0.3
              0.2   FLORAL
SWEET   0.1
                               SPICY

SMOKE   HERBAL/GRASSY

PEAT   TOFFEE   MALT/CEREAL

NOTES:

. . . .
. . . .
. . . .
. . . .
. . . .
. . . .

👉 **DISTILLER:** ....

AGE/EXPRESSION: ....

ORIGIN: .... **PRICE:** ....

SAMPLED: .... **RATING:** ☆ ☆ ☆ ☆ ☆

COLOR METER:

- MAHOGANY
- CARAMEL
- AMBER
- GOLD
- HONEY
- STRAW
- CLEAR

FLAVOR WHEEL:

HEAT/ABV: _____ %

BALANCE · FINISH · DARK FRUIT · CITRUS FRUIT · FLORAL · SPICY · HERBAL/GRASSY · MALT/CEREAL · TOFFEE · PEAT · SMOKE · SWEET · SALTY · ASTRINGENT · BODY

0.1 0.2 0.3 0.4 0.5

NOTES:

....
....
....
....
....
....

☞ DISTILLER: ....

AGE/EXPRESSION: ....

ORIGIN: .... PRICE: ....

SAMPLED: .... RATING: ☆☆☆☆☆

COLOR METER: FLAVOR WHEEL:

COLOR METER:
- MAHOGANY
- CARAMEL
- AMBER
- GOLD
- HONEY
- STRAW
- CLEAR

HEAT/ABV: _____ %

FLAVOR WHEEL:
BALANCE · FINISH · DARK FRUIT · CITRUS FRUIT · FLORAL · SPICY · HERBAL/GRASSY · MALT/CEREAL · TOFFEE · PEAT · SMOKE · SWEET · SALTY · ASTRINGENT · BODY

#5 #4 #3 #2 #1

NOTES:
....
....
....
....
....

DISTILLER: ....

AGE/EXPRESSION: ....

ORIGIN: .... PRICE: ....

SAMPLED: .... RATING: ☆ ☆ ☆ ☆ ☆

COLOR METER:

- MAHOGANY
- CARAMEL
- AMBER
- GOLD
- HONEY
- STRAW
- CLEAR

FLAVOR WHEEL:

HEAT/ABV: _____ %

BALANCE · FINISH · DARK FRUIT · CITRUS FRUIT · FLORAL · SPICY · HERBAL/GRASSY · MALT/CEREAL · TOFFEE · PEAT · SMOKE · SWEET · SALTY · ASTRINGENT · BODY

0.5 0.4 0.3 0.2 0.1

NOTES:

....
....
....
....
....
....

☞ DISTILLER: . . . .

AGE/EXPRESSION: . . . .

ORIGIN: . . . .   PRICE: . . . .

SAMPLED: . . . .   RATING: ☆ ☆ ☆ ☆ ☆

COLOR METER:

- MAHOGANY
- CARAMEL
- AMBER
- GOLD
- HONEY
- STRAW
- CLEAR

FLAVOR WHEEL:

HEAT/ _____ %
ABV: _____

BALANCE — FINISH — DARK FRUIT

BODY — CITRUS FRUIT

ASTRIN-GENT — FLORAL

SALTY — SPICY

SWEET — HERBAL/GRASSY

SMOKE — MALT/CEREAL

PEAT — TOFFEE

(wheel rings labeled: 1, 2, 3, 4, 5)

NOTES:

. . . .

. . . .

. . . .

. . . .

. . . .

👉 **DISTILLER:** ....

AGE/EXPRESSION: ....

ORIGIN: .... **PRICE:** ....

SAMPLED: .... **RATING:** ☆☆☆☆☆

COLOR METER:

- MAHOGANY
- CARAMEL
- AMBER
- GOLD
- HONEY
- STRAW
- CLEAR

FLAVOR WHEEL:

HEAT/ABV: _____ %

BALANCE · FINISH · DARK FRUIT · CITRUS FRUIT · FLORAL · SPICY · HERBAL/GRASSY · MALT/CEREAL · TOFFEE · PEAT · SMOKE · SWEET · SALTY · ASTRINGENT · BODY

0.1 · 0.2 · 0.3 · 0.4 · 0.5

NOTES:

....
....
....
....
....
....

👉 **DISTILLER:** . . . .

AGE/EXPRESSION: . . . .

ORIGIN: . . . . **PRICE:** . . . .

SAMPLED: . . . . **RATING:** ☆ ☆ ☆ ☆ ☆

COLOR METER:

- MAHOGANY
- CARAMEL
- AMBER
- GOLD
- HONEY
- STRAW
- CLEAR

FLAVOR WHEEL:

HEAT/ABV: _____ %

BALANCE · FINISH · DARK FRUIT · CITRUS FRUIT · FLORAL · SPICY · HERBAL/GRASSY · MALT/CEREAL · TOFFEE · PEAT · SMOKE · SWEET · SALTY · ASTRIN-GENT · BODY

0.1 0.2 0.3 0.4 0.5

NOTES:

. . . .

. . . .

. . . .

. . . .

. . . .

☜ **DISTILLER:** ....

AGE/EXPRESSION: ....

ORIGIN: .... **PRICE:** ....

SAMPLED: .... **RATING:** ☆☆☆☆☆

COLOR METER:

- MAHOGANY
- CARAMEL
- AMBER
- GOLD
- HONEY
- STRAW
- CLEAR

FLAVOR WHEEL:

HEAT/ABV : _____ %

FINISH
BALANCE
BODY
DARK FRUIT
ASTRIN-GENT
CITRUS FRUIT
SALTY
FLORAL
SWEET
SPICY
SMOKE
HERBAL/GRASSY
PEAT
TOFFEE
MALT/CEREAL

0.1 0.2 0.3 0.4 0.5

NOTES: ....
....
....
....
....
....

👉 DISTILLER: . . . .

AGE/EXPRESSION: . . . .

ORIGIN: . . . . PRICE: . . . .

SAMPLED: . . . . RATING: ☆ ☆ ☆ ☆ ☆

COLOR METER:

- MAHOGANY
- CARAMEL
- AMBER
- GOLD
- HONEY
- STRAW
- CLEAR

FLAVOR WHEEL:

HEAT/ %
ABV: . . . .

BALANCE
BODY
ASTRIN-
GENT
SALTY
SWEET
SMOKE
PEAT
FINISH
TOFFEE
MALT/
CEREAL
HERBAL/
GRASSY
SPICY
FLORAL
CITRUS
FRUIT
DARK FRUIT

0.5
0.4
0.3
0.2
0.1

NOTES:

. . . .

. . . .

. . . .

. . . .

. . . .

. . . .

DISTILLER: . . . .

AGE/EXPRESSION: . . . .

ORIGIN: . . . . PRICE: . . . .

SAMPLED: . . . . RATING: ☆ ☆ ☆ ☆ ☆

COLOR METER:

- MAHOGANY
- CARAMEL
- AMBER
- GOLD
- HONEY
- STRAW
- CLEAR

FLAVOR WHEEL:

HEAT/ %
ABV: . . . .

BALANCE · FINISH
BODY · DARK FRUIT
ASTRIN-GENT · CITRUS FRUIT
SALTY · FLORAL
SWEET · SPICY
SMOKE · HERBAL/GRASSY
PEAT · TOFFEE · MALT/CEREAL

0.5
0.4
0.3
0.2
0.1

NOTES:

. . . .

. . . .

. . . .

. . . .

. . . .

👉 **DISTILLER:** . . . .

AGE/EXPRESSION: . . . .

ORIGIN: . . . .   **PRICE:** . . . .

SAMPLED: . . . .   **RATING:** ☆ ☆ ☆ ☆ ☆

COLOR METER:

- MAHOGANY
- CARAMEL
- AMBER
- GOLD
- HONEY
- STRAW
- CLEAR

FLAVOR WHEEL:

BALANCE FINISH

BODY DARK FRUIT

ASTRIN-GENT CITRUS FRUIT

SALTY FLORAL

SWEET SPICY

SMOKE HERBAL/GRASSY

PEAT TOFFEE MALT/CEREAL

0.1 0.2 0.3 0.4 0.5

HEAT/ABV: . . . . %

NOTES: . . . .

. . . .

. . . .

. . . .

. . . .

. . . .

👉 **DISTILLER:** ....

AGE/EXPRESSION: ....

ORIGIN: .... **PRICE:** ....

SAMPLED: .... **RATING:** ☆☆☆☆☆

COLOR METER:

- MAHOGANY
- CARAMEL
- AMBER
- GOLD
- HONEY
- STRAW
- CLEAR

FLAVOR WHEEL:

HEAT/
ABV : _____ %

BALANCE · FINISH · DARK FRUIT · CITRUS FRUIT · FLORAL · SPICY · HERBAL/GRASSY · MALT/CEREAL · TOFFEE · PEAT · SMOKE · SWEET · SALTY · ASTRIN-GENT · BODY

0.1 0.2 0.3 0.4 0.5

NOTES:
....
....
....
....
....
....

👉 DISTILLER: ....

AGE/EXPRESSION: ....

ORIGIN: .... PRICE: ....

SAMPLED: .... RATING: ☆☆☆☆☆

COLOR METER: FLAVOR WHEEL:

MAHOGANY   HEAT/   %
                                            ABV: _____
CARAMEL   BALANCE   FINISH

                     BODY   DARK FRUIT
AMBER
                 ASTRIN-   0.5   CITRUS
GOLD   GENT   0.4   FRUIT
                          0.3
HONEY   SALTY   0.2   0.1   FLORAL

STRAW   SWEET   SPICY

CLEAR   SMOKE   HERBAL/
                                           GRASSY
                     PEAT   MALT/
                          TOFFEE   CEREAL

NOTES: ....
....
....
....
....
....

DISTILLER: ....

AGE/EXPRESSION: ....

ORIGIN: ....   **PRICE:** ....

SAMPLED: ....   **RATING:** ☆ ☆ ☆ ☆ ☆

COLOR METER:

- MAHOGANY
- CARAMEL
- AMBER
- GOLD
- HONEY
- STRAW
- CLEAR

FLAVOR WHEEL:

HEAT/ABV: _____ %

BALANCE · FINISH · DARK FRUIT · CITRUS FRUIT · FLORAL · SPICY · HERBAL/GRASSY · MALT/CEREAL · TOFFEE · PEAT · SMOKE · SWEET · SALTY · ASTRINGENT · BODY

0.1 0.2 0.3 0.4 0.5

NOTES: ....
....
....
....
....
....

☞ **DISTILLER:** . . . .

AGE/EXPRESSION: . . . .

ORIGIN: . . . .   **PRICE:** . . . .

SAMPLED: . . . .   **RATING:** ☆ ☆ ☆ ☆ ☆

COLOR METER:

- MAHOGANY
- CARAMEL
- AMBER
- GOLD
- HONEY
- STRAW
- CLEAR

FLAVOR WHEEL:

HEAT/   %
ABV: _____

FINISH
BALANCE
BODY
ASTRIN-GENT
SALTY
SWEET
SMOKE
PEAT
TOFFEE
MALT/CEREAL
HERBAL/GRASSY
SPICY
FLORAL
CITRUS FRUIT
DARK FRUIT

0.5
0.4
0.3
0.2
0.1

NOTES:

. . . .

☞ **DISTILLER:** . . . .

AGE/EXPRESSION: . . . .

ORIGIN: . . . . **PRICE:** . . . .

SAMPLED: . . . . **RATING:** ☆ ☆ ☆ ☆ ☆

COLOR METER:

- MAHOGANY
- CARAMEL
- AMBER
- GOLD
- HONEY
- STRAW
- CLEAR

FLAVOR WHEEL:

HEAT/ABV : _____ %

FINISH
BALANCE
BODY
DARK FRUIT
ASTRIN-GENT
CITRUS FRUIT
SALTY
FLORAL
SWEET
SPICY
SMOKE
HERBAL/GRASSY
PEAT
TOFFEE
MALT/CEREAL

0.5
0.4
0.3
0.2
0.1

NOTES:
. . . .
. . . .
. . . .
. . . .
. . . .
. . . .

👉 DISTILLER: . . . .

AGE/EXPRESSION: . . . .

ORIGIN: . . . . PRICE: . . . .

SAMPLED: . . . . RATING: ☆ ☆ ☆ ☆ ☆

COLOR METER:

- MAHOGANY
- CARAMEL
- AMBER
- GOLD
- HONEY
- STRAW
- CLEAR

FLAVOR WHEEL:

HEAT/ABV: . . . . %

BALANCE
FINISH
BODY
DARK FRUIT
ASTRIN-GENT
CITRUS FRUIT
SALTY
FLORAL
SWEET
SPICY
SMOKE
HERBAL/GRASSY
PEAT
MALT/CEREAL
TOFFEE

0.5
0.4
0.3
0.2
0.1

NOTES:

. . . .

. . . .

. . . .

. . . .

. . . .

DISTILLER: ....

AGE/EXPRESSION: ....

ORIGIN: ....   PRICE: ....

SAMPLED: ....   RATING: ☆ ☆ ☆ ☆ ☆

COLOR METER:

- MAHOGANY
- CARAMEL
- AMBER
- GOLD
- HONEY
- STRAW
- CLEAR

FLAVOR WHEEL:

HEAT/ABV: _____ %

BALANCE FINISH

BODY DARK FRUIT

ASTRIN-GENT CITRUS FRUIT

SALTY FLORAL

SWEET SPICY

SMOKE HERBAL/GRASSY

PEAT TOFFEE MALT/CEREAL

0.1 0.2 0.3 0.4 0.5

NOTES:

....
....
....
....
....
....

☞ **DISTILLER:** . . . .

AGE/EXPRESSION: . . . .

ORIGIN: . . . .   **PRICE:** . . . .

SAMPLED: . . . .   **RATING:** ☆ ☆ ☆ ☆ ☆

COLOR METER:

- MAHOGANY
- CARAMEL
- AMBER
- GOLD
- HONEY
- STRAW
- CLEAR

FLAVOR WHEEL:

BALANCE   FINISH

BODY   DARK FRUIT

ASTRIN-GENT   CITRUS FRUIT

SALTY   FLORAL

SWEET   SPICY

SMOKE   HERBAL/GRASSY

PEAT   TOFFEE   MALT/CEREAL

0.5   0.4   0.3   0.2   0.1

HEAT/ABV: _____ %

NOTES:

. . . .

. . . .

. . . .

. . . .

. . . .

👉 **DISTILLER:** ....

AGE/EXPRESSION: ....

ORIGIN: .... **PRICE:** ....

SAMPLED: .... **RATING:** ☆☆☆☆☆

COLOR METER:

- MAHOGANY
- CARAMEL
- AMBER
- GOLD
- HONEY
- STRAW
- CLEAR

FLAVOR WHEEL:

HEAT/ABV: _____ %

BALANCE · FINISH · DARK FRUIT · CITRUS FRUIT · FLORAL · SPICY · HERBAL/GRASSY · MALT/CEREAL · TOFFEE · PEAT · SMOKE · SWEET · SALTY · ASTRINGENT · BODY

0.5 0.4 0.3 0.2 0.1

NOTES:

....

....

....

....

....

☞ DISTILLER: . . . .

AGE/EXPRESSION: . . . .

ORIGIN: . . . . PRICE: . . . .

SAMPLED: . . . . RATING: ☆ ☆ ☆ ☆ ☆

COLOR METER:

- MAHOGANY
- CARAMEL
- AMBER
- GOLD
- HONEY
- STRAW
- CLEAR

FLAVOR WHEEL:

HEAT/   %
ABV: . . . .

BALANCE   FINISH

BODY

ASTRIN-GENT

SALTY

SWEET

SMOKE

PEAT   TOFFEE   MALT/CEREAL

HERBAL/GRASSY

SPICY

FLORAL

CITRUS FRUIT

DARK FRUIT

0.5
0.4
0.3
0.2
0.1

NOTES:

. . . .

. . . .

. . . .

. . . .

. . . .

☞ **DISTILLER:** . . . .

AGE/EXPRESSION: . . . .

ORIGIN: . . . .   **PRICE:** . . . .

SAMPLED: . . . .   **RATING:** ☆ ☆ ☆ ☆ ☆

COLOR METER:

- MAHOGANY
- CARAMEL
- AMBER
- GOLD
- HONEY
- STRAW
- CLEAR

FLAVOR WHEEL:

HEAT/ ABV : . . . . %

BALANCE
FINISH
BODY
DARK FRUIT
ASTRIN-GENT
CITRUS FRUIT
SALTY
FLORAL
SWEET
SPICY
SMOKE
HERBAL/ GRASSY
PEAT
TOFFEE
MALT/ CEREAL

0.5
0.4
0.3
0.2
0.1

NOTES:

. . . .

. . . .

. . . .

. . . .

. . . .

☞ **DISTILLER:** . . . .

AGE/EXPRESSION: . . . .

ORIGIN: . . . .   **PRICE:** . . . .

SAMPLED: . . . .   **RATING:** ☆ ☆ ☆ ☆ ☆

COLOR METER:

- MAHOGANY
- CARAMEL
- AMBER
- GOLD
- HONEY
- STRAW
- CLEAR

FLAVOR WHEEL:

HEAT/   %
ABV: _____

FINISH, BALANCE, BODY, ASTRINGENT, SALTY, SWEET, SMOKE, PEAT, TOFFEE, MALT/CEREAL, HERBAL/GRASSY, SPICY, FLORAL, CITRUS FRUIT, DARK FRUIT

0.1 0.2 0.3 0.4 0.5

NOTES:

. . . .

. . . .

. . . .

. . . .

. . . .

DISTILLER: ....

AGE/EXPRESSION: ....

ORIGIN: .... PRICE: ....

SAMPLED: .... RATING: ☆☆☆☆☆

COLOR METER:

- MAHOGANY
- CARAMEL
- AMBER
- GOLD
- HONEY
- STRAW
- CLEAR

FLAVOR WHEEL:

HEAT/ ABV: _____ %

BALANCE · FINISH · DARK FRUIT · CITRUS FRUIT · FLORAL · SPICY · HERBAL/GRASSY · MALT/CEREAL · TOFFEE · PEAT · SMOKE · SWEET · SALTY · ASTRIN-GENT · BODY

0.5 0.4 0.3 0.2 0.1

NOTES:

....
....
....
....
....
....

☞ DISTILLER: . . . .

AGE/EXPRESSION: . . . .

ORIGIN: . . . .   PRICE: . . . .

SAMPLED: . . . .   RATING: ☆ ☆ ☆ ☆ ☆

COLOR METER:

- MAHOGANY
- CARAMEL
- AMBER
- GOLD
- HONEY
- STRAW
- CLEAR

FLAVOR WHEEL:

HEAT/ABV: . . . . %

BALANCE · FINISH · DARK FRUIT · CITRUS FRUIT · FLORAL · SPICY · HERBAL/GRASSY · MALT/CEREAL · TOFFEE · PEAT · SMOKE · SWEET · SALTY · ASTRIN-GENT · BODY

0.1 0.2 0.3 0.4 0.5

NOTES:

. . . .
. . . .
. . . .
. . . .
. . . .
. . . .

☞ DISTILLER: . . . .

AGE/EXPRESSION: . . . .

ORIGIN: . . . . PRICE: . . . .

SAMPLED: . . . . RATING: ☆ ☆ ☆ ☆ ☆

COLOR METER:

- MAHOGANY
- CARAMEL
- AMBER
- GOLD
- HONEY
- STRAW
- CLEAR

FLAVOR WHEEL:

HEAT/ABV: . . . . %

BALANCE, FINISH, BODY, DARK FRUIT, ASTRINGENT, CITRUS FRUIT, SALTY, FLORAL, SWEET, SPICY, SMOKE, HERBAL/GRASSY, PEAT, TOFFEE, MALT/CEREAL

0.1 0.2 0.3 0.4 0.5

NOTES:

. . . .

. . . .

. . . .

. . . .

. . . .

👉 **DISTILLER:** . . . .

AGE/EXPRESSION: . . . .

ORIGIN: . . . . **PRICE:** . . . .

SAMPLED: . . . . **RATING:** ☆ ☆ ☆ ☆ ☆

COLOR METER:

- MAHOGANY
- CARAMEL
- AMBER
- GOLD
- HONEY
- STRAW
- CLEAR

FLAVOR WHEEL:

HEAT/ _____ %
ABV : _____

BALANCE FINISH
BODY
ASTRIN-GENT   DARK FRUIT
SALTY   CITRUS FRUIT
SWEET   FLORAL
SMOKE   SPICY
PEAT   HERBAL/GRASSY
TOFFEE MALT/CEREAL

0.5 0.4 0.3 0.2 0.1

NOTES:

. . . .

. . . .

. . . .

. . . .

. . . .

. . . .

DISTILLER: ....

AGE/EXPRESSION: ....

ORIGIN: .... **PRICE:** ....

SAMPLED: .... **RATING:** ☆☆☆☆☆

COLOR METER:

- MAHOGANY
- CARAMEL
- AMBER
- GOLD
- HONEY
- STRAW
- CLEAR

FLAVOR WHEEL:

HEAT/ABV: _____ %

BALANCE • FINISH • DARK FRUIT • CITRUS FRUIT • FLORAL • SPICY • HERBAL/GRASSY • MALT/CEREAL • TOFFEE • PEAT • SMOKE • SWEET • SALTY • ASTRINGENT • BODY

0.1 0.2 0.3 0.4 0.5

NOTES:

....
....
....
....
....
....

👉 **DISTILLER:** ....

AGE/EXPRESSION: ....

ORIGIN: .... **PRICE:** ....

SAMPLED: .... **RATING:** ☆ ☆ ☆ ☆ ☆

COLOR METER:

- MAHOGANY
- CARAMEL
- AMBER
- GOLD
- HONEY
- STRAW
- CLEAR

FLAVOR WHEEL:

HEAT/ABV : _____ %

BALANCE
FINISH
BODY
DARK FRUIT
ASTRIN-GENT
CITRUS FRUIT
SALTY
FLORAL
SWEET
SPICY
SMOKE
HERBAL/GRASSY
PEAT
TOFFEE
MALT/CEREAL

0.5 0.4 0.3 0.2 0.1

NOTES:

....
....
....
....
....

DISTILLER: ....

AGE/EXPRESSION: ....

ORIGIN: .... PRICE: ....

SAMPLED: .... RATING: ☆ ☆ ☆ ☆ ☆

COLOR METER:

- MAHOGANY
- CARAMEL
- AMBER
- GOLD
- HONEY
- STRAW
- CLEAR

FLAVOR WHEEL:

HEAT / ABV: _____ %

BALANCE
FINISH
BODY
DARK FRUIT
ASTRIN-GENT
CITRUS FRUIT
SALTY
FLORAL
SWEET
SPICY
SMOKE
HERBAL/ GRASSY
PEAT
TOFFEE
MALT/ CEREAL

0.5
0.4
0.3
0.2
0.1

NOTES:

....
....
....
....
....
....

☞ **DISTILLER:** . . . .

AGE/EXPRESSION: . . . .

ORIGIN: . . . . **PRICE:** . . . .

SAMPLED: . . . . **RATING:** ☆ ☆ ☆ ☆ ☆

COLOR METER:

- MAHOGANY
- CARAMEL
- AMBER
- GOLD
- HONEY
- STRAW
- CLEAR

FLAVOR WHEEL:

HEAT/ %
ABV: . . . .

BALANCE
BODY
ASTRIN-GENT
SALTY
SWEET
SMOKE
PEAT
FINISH
0.5
0.4
0.3
0.2
0.1
DARK FRUIT
CITRUS FRUIT
FLORAL
SPICY
HERBAL/ GRASSY
MALT/ CEREAL
TOFFEE

NOTES:

. . . .

. . . .

. . . .

. . . .

. . . .

. . . .

👉 **DISTILLER:** ....

AGE/EXPRESSION: ....

ORIGIN: .... **PRICE:** ....

SAMPLED: .... **RATING:** ☆ ☆ ☆ ☆ ☆

COLOR METER:

- MAHOGANY
- CARAMEL
- AMBER
- GOLD
- HONEY
- STRAW
- CLEAR

FLAVOR WHEEL:

HEAT/
ABV: _____ %

BALANCE · FINISH · DARK FRUIT · CITRUS FRUIT · FLORAL · SPICY · HERBAL/GRASSY · MALT/CEREAL · TOFFEE · PEAT · SMOKE · SWEET · SALTY · ASTRINGENT · BODY

0.5 · 0.4 · 0.3 · 0.2 · 0.1

NOTES:

....

....

....

....

....

....

DISTILLER: ....

AGE/EXPRESSION: ....

ORIGIN: .... **PRICE:** ....

SAMPLED: .... **RATING:** ☆ ☆ ☆ ☆ ☆

COLOR METER:

- MAHOGANY
- CARAMEL
- AMBER
- GOLD
- HONEY
- STRAW
- CLEAR

FLAVOR WHEEL:

HEAT/ ABV: _____ %

BALANCE
FINISH
BODY
DARK FRUIT
ASTRIN-GENT
CITRUS FRUIT
SALTY
FLORAL
SWEET
SPICY
SMOKE
HERBAL/ GRASSY
PEAT
MALT/ CEREAL
TOFFEE

NOTES:

....
....
....
....
....
....

👉 **DISTILLER:** ....

AGE/EXPRESSION: ....

ORIGIN: .... **PRICE:** ....

SAMPLED: .... **RATING:** ☆ ☆ ☆ ☆ ☆

COLOR METER:

- MAHOGANY
- CARAMEL
- AMBER
- GOLD
- HONEY
- STRAW
- CLEAR

FLAVOR WHEEL:

HEAT/ABV: _____ %

BALANCE — FINISH — DARK FRUIT — CITRUS FRUIT — FLORAL — SPICY — HERBAL/GRASSY — MALT/CEREAL — TOFFEE — PEAT — SMOKE — SWEET — SALTY — ASTRINGENT — BODY

0.1 0.2 0.3 0.4 0.5

NOTES:
....
....
....
....
....
....

☞ **DISTILLER:** ....

AGE/EXPRESSION: ....

ORIGIN: .... **PRICE:** ....

SAMPLED: .... **RATING:** ☆☆☆☆☆

COLOR METER:

- MAHOGANY
- CARAMEL
- AMBER
- GOLD
- HONEY
- STRAW
- CLEAR

FLAVOR WHEEL:

HEAT/ ABV: _____ %

FINISH
BALANCE
BODY
DARK FRUIT
ASTRIN-GENT
CITRUS FRUIT
SALTY
FLORAL
SWEET
SPICY
SMOKE
HERBAL/ GRASSY
PEAT
TOFFEE
MALT/ CEREAL

0.5
0.4
0.3
0.2
0.1

NOTES:

....
....
....
....
....
....

👉 DISTILLER: ....

AGE/EXPRESSION: ....

ORIGIN: ....   PRICE: ....

SAMPLED: ....   RATING: ☆☆☆☆☆

COLOR METER:

- MAHOGANY
- CARAMEL
- AMBER
- GOLD
- HONEY
- STRAW
- CLEAR

FLAVOR WHEEL:

HEAT/ABV: _____ %

FINISH
BALANCE
BODY
ASTRIN-GENT
SALTY
SWEET
SMOKE
PEAT
TOFFEE
MALT/CEREAL
HERBAL/GRASSY
SPICY
FLORAL
CITRUS FRUIT
DARK FRUIT

0.1 0.2 0.3 0.4 0.5

NOTES:
....
....
....
....
....
....

DISTILLER: ....

AGE/EXPRESSION: ....

ORIGIN: .... PRICE: ....

SAMPLED: .... RATING: ☆ ☆ ☆ ☆ ☆

COLOR METER:

- MAHOGANY
- CARAMEL
- AMBER
- GOLD
- HONEY
- STRAW
- CLEAR

FLAVOR WHEEL:

HEAT/ABV: _____ %

BALANCE
FINISH
BODY
DARK FRUIT
ASTRIN-GENT
CITRUS FRUIT
SALTY
FLORAL
SWEET
SPICY
SMOKE
HERBAL/GRASSY
PEAT
TOFFEE
MALT/CEREAL

0.1 0.2 0.3 0.4 0.5

NOTES:

....

....

....

....

....

....

DISTILLER: ....

AGE/EXPRESSION: ....

ORIGIN: .... PRICE: ....

SAMPLED: .... RATING: ☆ ☆ ☆ ☆ ☆

COLOR METER:

- MAHOGANY
- CARAMEL
- AMBER
- GOLD
- HONEY
- STRAW
- CLEAR

FLAVOR WHEEL:

HEAT/ABV: .... %

BALANCE
FINISH
BODY
DARK FRUIT
ASTRIN-GENT
CITRUS FRUIT
SALTY
FLORAL
SWEET
SPICY
SMOKE
HERBAL/GRASSY
PEAT
TOFFEE
MALT/CEREAL

0.5 0.4 0.3 0.2 0.1

NOTES: ....
....
....
....
....
....

☞ **DISTILLER:** . . . .

AGE/EXPRESSION: . . . .

ORIGIN: . . . . **PRICE:** . . . .

SAMPLED: . . . . **RATING:** ☆☆☆☆☆

COLOR METER:

- MAHOGANY
- CARAMEL
- AMBER
- GOLD
- HONEY
- STRAW
- CLEAR

FLAVOR WHEEL:

HEAT/ABV: _____ %

FINISH
BALANCE
BODY
ASTRIN-GENT
SALTY
SWEET
SMOKE
PEAT
TOFFEE
MALT/CEREAL
HERBAL/GRASSY
SPICY
FLORAL
CITRUS FRUIT
DARK FRUIT

0.1 0.2 0.3 0.4 0.5

NOTES: . . . .

. . . .

. . . .

. . . .

. . . .

. . . .

👉 **DISTILLER:** . . . .

AGE/EXPRESSION: . . . .

ORIGIN: . . . . **PRICE:** . . . .

SAMPLED: . . . . **RATING:** ☆ ☆ ☆ ☆ ☆

COLOR METER:

- MAHOGANY
- CARAMEL
- AMBER
- GOLD
- HONEY
- STRAW
- CLEAR

FLAVOR WHEEL:

HEAT/ABV: _____ %

BALANCE · FINISH · DARK FRUIT · CITRUS FRUIT · FLORAL · SPICY · HERBAL/GRASSY · MALT/CEREAL · TOFFEE · PEAT · SMOKE · SWEET · SALTY · ASTRINGENT · BODY

0.5
0.4
0.3
0.2
0.1

NOTES:

. . . .

. . . .

. . . .

. . . .

. . . .

. . . .

☞ **DISTILLER:** . . . .

AGE/EXPRESSION: . . . .

ORIGIN: . . . . **PRICE:** . . . .

SAMPLED: . . . . **RATING:** ☆ ☆ ☆ ☆ ☆

COLOR METER:

- MAHOGANY
- CARAMEL
- AMBER
- GOLD
- HONEY
- STRAW
- CLEAR

FLAVOR WHEEL:

HEAT/ABV: . . . . %

BALANCE · FINISH · DARK FRUIT · CITRUS FRUIT · FLORAL · SPICY · HERBAL/GRASSY · MALT/CEREAL · TOFFEE · PEAT · SMOKE · SWEET · SALTY · ASTRINGENT · BODY

0.1 0.2 0.3 0.4 0.5

NOTES:

. . . .

. . . .

. . . .

. . . .

. . . .

👉 **DISTILLER:** . . . .

AGE/EXPRESSION: . . . .

ORIGIN: . . . . **PRICE:** . . . .

SAMPLED: . . . . **RATING:** ☆ ☆ ☆ ☆ ☆

COLOR METER:

- MAHOGANY
- CARAMEL
- AMBER
- GOLD
- HONEY
- STRAW
- CLEAR

FLAVOR WHEEL:

HEAT/ABV : . . . . %

BALANCE · FINISH · DARK FRUIT · CITRUS FRUIT · FLORAL · SPICY · HERBAL/GRASSY · MALT/CEREAL · TOFFEE · PEAT · SMOKE · SWEET · SALTY · ASTRINGENT · BODY

0.5 0.4 0.3 0.2 0.1

NOTES: . . . .

. . . .

. . . .

. . . .

. . . .

. . . .

👉 DISTILLER: . . . .

AGE/EXPRESSION: . . . .

ORIGIN: . . . . PRICE: . . . .

SAMPLED: . . . . RATING: ☆ ☆ ☆ ☆ ☆

COLOR METER:

- MAHOGANY
- CARAMEL
- AMBER
- GOLD
- HONEY
- STRAW
- CLEAR

FLAVOR WHEEL:

HEAT/   %
ABV: . . . .

BALANCE   FINISH

BODY   DARK FRUIT

ASTRIN-GENT   CITRUS FRUIT

SALTY   FLORAL

SWEET   SPICY

SMOKE   HERBAL/GRASSY

PEAT   TOFFEE   MALT/CEREAL

(wheel scale: 0.1, 0.2, 0.3, 0.4, 0.5)

NOTES:

. . . .

. . . .

. . . .

. . . .

. . . .

. . . .

👉 **DISTILLER:** ....

AGE/EXPRESSION: ....

ORIGIN: .... **PRICE:** ....

SAMPLED: .... **RATING:** ☆ ☆ ☆ ☆ ☆

COLOR METER:

- MAHOGANY
- CARAMEL
- AMBER
- GOLD
- HONEY
- STRAW
- CLEAR

FLAVOR WHEEL:

HEAT/ %
ABV : _____

BALANCE — FINISH — DARK FRUIT

BODY — CITRUS FRUIT

ASTRIN-GENT — FLORAL

SALTY — SPICY

SWEET — HERBAL/GRASSY

SMOKE — MALT/CEREAL

PEAT — TOFFEE

(0.1, 0.2, 0.3, 0.4, 0.5)

NOTES: ....
....
....
....
....
....

👉 **DISTILLER:** ....

AGE/EXPRESSION: ....

ORIGIN: .... **PRICE:** ....

SAMPLED: .... **RATING:** ☆ ☆ ☆ ☆ ☆

COLOR METER:

- MAHOGANY
- CARAMEL
- AMBER
- GOLD
- HONEY
- STRAW
- CLEAR

FLAVOR WHEEL:

HEAT/ABV: _____ %

BALANCE, FINISH, BODY, DARK FRUIT, ASTRINGENT, CITRUS FRUIT, SALTY, FLORAL, SWEET, SPICY, SMOKE, HERBAL/GRASSY, PEAT, TOFFEE, MALT/CEREAL

0.1 0.2 0.3 0.4 0.5

NOTES: ....

....

....

....

....

....

👉 DISTILLER: . . . .

AGE/EXPRESSION: . . . .

ORIGIN: . . . .   PRICE: . . . .

SAMPLED: . . . .   RATING: ☆ ☆ ☆ ☆ ☆

COLOR METER:

- MAHOGANY
- CARAMEL
- AMBER
- GOLD
- HONEY
- STRAW
- CLEAR

FLAVOR WHEEL:

HEAT/ _____ %
ABV : _____

BALANCE   FINISH

BODY   DARK FRUIT

ASTRIN-GENT   CITRUS FRUIT

0.5
0.4
0.3
0.2
0.1

SALTY   FLORAL

SWEET   SPICY

SMOKE   HERBAL/ GRASSY

PEAT   TOFFEE   MALT/ CEREAL

NOTES:

. . . .

. . . .

. . . .

. . . .

. . . .

👉 **DISTILLER:** . . . .

AGE/EXPRESSION: . . . .

ORIGIN: . . . .   **PRICE:** . . . .

SAMPLED: . . . .   **RATING:** ☆ ☆ ☆ ☆ ☆

COLOR METER:

- MAHOGANY
- CARAMEL
- AMBER
- GOLD
- HONEY
- STRAW
- CLEAR

FLAVOR WHEEL:

HEAT / ABV: _____ %

BALANCE · FINISH · DARK FRUIT · CITRUS FRUIT · FLORAL · SPICY · HERBAL/ GRASSY · MALT/ CEREAL · TOFFEE · PEAT · SMOKE · SWEET · SALTY · ASTRIN-GENT · BODY

0.1 0.2 0.3 0.4 0.5

NOTES:

. . . .

. . . .

. . . .

. . . .

. . . .

. . . .

DISTILLER: ....

AGE/EXPRESSION: ....

ORIGIN: .... **PRICE:** ....

SAMPLED: .... **RATING:** ☆ ☆ ☆ ☆ ☆

COLOR METER:

- MAHOGANY
- CARAMEL
- AMBER
- GOLD
- HONEY
- STRAW
- CLEAR

FLAVOR WHEEL:

HEAT/ABV: _____ %

BALANCE · FINISH · DARK FRUIT · CITRUS FRUIT · FLORAL · SPICY · HERBAL/GRASSY · MALT/CEREAL · TOFFEE · PEAT · SMOKE · SWEET · SALTY · ASTRINGENT · BODY

0.1 0.2 0.3 0.4 0.5

NOTES:

....
....
....
....
....
....

☞ DISTILLER: ....

AGE/EXPRESSION: ....

ORIGIN: .... PRICE: ....

SAMPLED: .... RATING: ☆☆☆☆☆

COLOR METER:

- MAHOGANY
- CARAMEL
- AMBER
- GOLD
- HONEY
- STRAW
- CLEAR

FLAVOR WHEEL:

HEAT/ABV: _____ %

BALANCE
FINISH
BODY
DARK FRUIT
ASTRIN-GENT
CITRUS FRUIT
SALTY
FLORAL
SWEET
SPICY
SMOKE
HERBAL/GRASSY
PEAT
TOFFEE
MALT/CEREAL

0.1 0.2 0.3 0.4 0.5

NOTES:

....
....
....
....
....
....

👉 DISTILLER: ....

AGE/EXPRESSION: ....

ORIGIN: .... PRICE: ....

SAMPLED: .... RATING: ☆ ☆ ☆ ☆ ☆

COLOR METER:

- MAHOGANY
- CARAMEL
- AMBER
- GOLD
- HONEY
- STRAW
- CLEAR

FLAVOR WHEEL:

HEAT/ ABV: _____ %

BALANCE
FINISH
BODY
DARK FRUIT
ASTRIN-GENT
CITRUS FRUIT
SALTY
FLORAL
SWEET
SPICY
SMOKE
HERBAL/ GRASSY
PEAT
TOFFEE
MALT/ CEREAL

0.5 0.4 0.3 0.2 0.1

NOTES:

....

....

....

....

....

....

👉 **DISTILLER:** ....

AGE/EXPRESSION: ....

ORIGIN: .... **PRICE:** ....

SAMPLED: .... **RATING:** ☆☆☆☆☆

COLOR METER:

- MAHOGANY
- CARAMEL
- AMBER
- GOLD
- HONEY
- STRAW
- CLEAR

FLAVOR WHEEL:

HEAT / ABV: _____ %

BALANCE
FINISH
BODY
DARK FRUIT
ASTRIN-GENT
CITRUS FRUIT
SALTY
FLORAL
SWEET
SPICY
SMOKE
HERBAL/ GRASSY
PEAT
TOFFEE
MALT/ CEREAL

0.5 0.4 0.3 0.2 0.1

NOTES:

....
....
....
....
....
....

☞ **DISTILLER:** . . . .

AGE/EXPRESSION: . . . .

ORIGIN: . . . .   **PRICE:** . . . .

SAMPLED: . . . .   **RATING:** ☆ ☆ ☆ ☆ ☆

COLOR METER:

- MAHOGANY
- CARAMEL
- AMBER
- GOLD
- HONEY
- STRAW
- CLEAR

FLAVOR WHEEL:

HEAT/ABV: _____ %

BALANCE, FINISH, BODY, DARK FRUIT, ASTRINGENT, CITRUS FRUIT, SALTY, FLORAL, SWEET, SPICY, SMOKE, HERBAL/GRASSY, PEAT, TOFFEE, MALT/CEREAL

0.1 0.2 0.3 0.4 0.5

NOTES:

. . . .

. . . .

. . . .

. . . .

. . . .

👉 **DISTILLER:** . . . .

AGE/EXPRESSION: . . . .

ORIGIN: . . . . **PRICE:** . . . .

SAMPLED: . . . . **RATING:** ☆☆☆☆☆

COLOR METER:

- MAHOGANY
- CARAMEL
- AMBER
- GOLD
- HONEY
- STRAW
- CLEAR

FLAVOR WHEEL:

HEAT/ %
ABV: . . . .

BALANCE   FINISH

BODY   DARK FRUIT

ASTRIN-   CITRUS
GENT   FRUIT

SALTY   FLORAL

SWEET   SPICY

SMOKE   HERBAL/
                         GRASSY

PEAT   TOFFEE   MALT/
                  CEREAL

5 4 3 2 1

NOTES:

. . . .

. . . .

. . . .

. . . .

. . . .

. . . .

👉 **DISTILLER:** ....

AGE/EXPRESSION: ....

ORIGIN: .... **PRICE:** ....

SAMPLED: .... **RATING:** ☆ ☆ ☆ ☆ ☆

COLOR METER:

MAHOGANY

CARAMEL

AMBER

GOLD

HONEY

STRAW

CLEAR

FLAVOR WHEEL:

HEAT/ ABV: _____ %

BALANCE   FINISH

BODY   DARK FRUIT

ASTRIN-GENT   CITRUS FRUIT

SALTY   FLORAL

SWEET   SPICY

SMOKE   HERBAL/ GRASSY

PEAT   TOFFEE   MALT/ CEREAL

0.1 0.2 0.3 0.4 0.5

NOTES:

....

....

....

....

....

....

👉 **DISTILLER:** ....

AGE/EXPRESSION: ....

ORIGIN: .... **PRICE:** ....

SAMPLED: .... **RATING:** ☆☆☆☆☆

COLOR METER:

- MAHOGANY
- CARAMEL
- AMBER
- GOLD
- HONEY
- STRAW
- CLEAR

FLAVOR WHEEL:

HEAT/ABV: _____ %

BALANCE · FINISH · DARK FRUIT · CITRUS FRUIT · FLORAL · SPICY · HERBAL/GRASSY · MALT/CEREAL · TOFFEE · PEAT · SMOKE · SWEET · SALTY · ASTRINGENT · BODY

0.1 0.2 0.3 0.4 0.5

NOTES:

....
....
....
....
....
....

👉 **DISTILLER:** ....

AGE/EXPRESSION: ....

ORIGIN: .... **PRICE:** ....

SAMPLED: .... **RATING:** ☆☆☆☆☆

COLOR METER:

- MAHOGANY
- CARAMEL
- AMBER
- GOLD
- HONEY
- STRAW
- CLEAR

FLAVOR WHEEL:

HEAT / ABV: _____ %

BALANCE
FINISH
BODY
DARK FRUIT
ASTRIN-GENT
CITRUS FRUIT
SALTY
FLORAL
SWEET
SPICY
SMOKE
HERBAL/ GRASSY
PEAT
TOFFEE
MALT/ CEREAL

0.1 0.2 0.3 0.4 0.5

NOTES:

....

....

....

....

....

....

👉 **DISTILLER:** . . . .

AGE/EXPRESSION: . . . .

ORIGIN: . . . . **PRICE:** . . . .

SAMPLED: . . . . **RATING:** ☆ ☆ ☆ ☆ ☆

COLOR METER:

MAHOGANY

CARAMEL

AMBER

GOLD

HONEY

STRAW

CLEAR

FLAVOR WHEEL:

HEAT/ABV: _____ %

BALANCE   FINISH

BODY

ASTRIN-GENT   DARK FRUIT

SALTY   CITRUS FRUIT

SWEET   FLORAL

SMOKE   SPICY

PEAT   TOFFEE   MALT/CEREAL   HERBAL/GRASSY

0.1 0.2 0.3 0.4 0.5

NOTES:

. . . .
. . . .
. . . .
. . . .
. . . .
. . . .

DISTILLER: ....

AGE/EXPRESSION: ....

ORIGIN: .... PRICE: ....

SAMPLED: .... RATING: ☆☆☆☆☆

COLOR METER:

- MAHOGANY
- CARAMEL
- AMBER
- GOLD
- HONEY
- STRAW
- CLEAR

FLAVOR WHEEL:

HEAT/ABV: _____ %

FINISH
BALANCE
BODY
DARK FRUIT
ASTRIN-GENT
CITRUS FRUIT
SALTY
FLORAL
SWEET
SPICY
SMOKE
HERBAL/GRASSY
PEAT
TOFFEE
MALT/CEREAL

0.5 0.4 0.3 0.2 0.1

NOTES:
....
....
....
....
....

☞ DISTILLER: ....

AGE/EXPRESSION: ....

ORIGIN: .... PRICE: ....

SAMPLED: .... RATING: ☆☆☆☆☆

COLOR METER:

- MAHOGANY
- CARAMEL
- AMBER
- GOLD
- HONEY
- STRAW
- CLEAR

FLAVOR WHEEL:

HEAT/ABV: _____ %

FINISH
BALANCE
BODY
DARK FRUIT
ASTRIN-GENT
CITRUS FRUIT
SALTY
FLORAL
SWEET
SPICY
SMOKE
HERBAL/GRASSY
PEAT
TOFFEE
MALT/CEREAL

NOTES:

....
....
....
....
....
....

👉 **DISTILLER:** . . . .

AGE/EXPRESSION: . . . .

ORIGIN: . . . .   **PRICE:** . . . .

SAMPLED: . . . .   **RATING:** ☆ ☆ ☆ ☆ ☆

COLOR METER:

- MAHOGANY
- CARAMEL
- AMBER
- GOLD
- HONEY
- STRAW
- CLEAR

FLAVOR WHEEL:

HEAT/
ABV: _____ %

BALANCE   FINISH

BODY   DARK FRUIT

ASTRIN-GENT   CITRUS FRUIT

SALTY   FLORAL

SWEET   SPICY

SMOKE   HERBAL/GRASSY

PEAT   TOFFEE   MALT/CEREAL

0.5 0.4 0.3 0.2 0.1

NOTES: . . . .

. . . .

. . . .

. . . .

. . . .

. . . .

👉 **DISTILLER:** ....

AGE/EXPRESSION: ....

ORIGIN: .... **PRICE:** ....

SAMPLED: .... **RATING:** ☆☆☆☆☆

COLOR METER:

- MAHOGANY
- CARAMEL
- AMBER
- GOLD
- HONEY
- STRAW
- CLEAR

FLAVOR WHEEL:

HEAT/ABV: _____ %

BALANCE
BODY
FINISH
ASTRINGENT
DARK FRUIT
SALTY
CITRUS FRUIT
SWEET
FLORAL
SMOKE
SPICY
PEAT
HERBAL/GRASSY
TOFFEE
MALT/CEREAL

0.1 0.2 0.3 0.4 0.5

NOTES:

....

....

....

....

....

....

DISTILLER: ....

AGE/EXPRESSION: ....

ORIGIN: .... **PRICE:** ....

SAMPLED: .... **RATING:** ☆ ☆ ☆ ☆ ☆

COLOR METER:

- MAHOGANY
- CARAMEL
- AMBER
- GOLD
- HONEY
- STRAW
- CLEAR

FLAVOR WHEEL:

HEAT / ABV: _____ %

BALANCE
FINISH
BODY
DARK FRUIT
ASTRIN-GENT
CITRUS FRUIT
SALTY
FLORAL
SWEET
SPICY
SMOKE
HERBAL/ GRASSY
PEAT
TOFFEE
MALT/ CEREAL

0.5 0.4 0.3 0.2 0.1

NOTES:

....

....

....

....

....

👉 **DISTILLER:** ....

AGE/EXPRESSION: ....

ORIGIN: .... **PRICE:** ....

SAMPLED: .... **RATING:** ☆☆☆☆☆

COLOR METER:

- MAHOGANY
- CARAMEL
- AMBER
- GOLD
- HONEY
- STRAW
- CLEAR

FLAVOR WHEEL:

HEAT/ ABV: _____ %

BALANCE · FINISH
BODY
ASTRIN-GENT · DARK FRUIT
SALTY · CITRUS FRUIT
SWEET · FLORAL
SMOKE · SPICY
PEAT · HERBAL/GRASSY
TOFFEE · MALT/CEREAL

0.1 0.2 0.3 0.4 0.5

NOTES:

....

....

....

....

....

....

DISTILLER: . . . .

AGE/EXPRESSION: . . . .

ORIGIN: . . . . **PRICE:** . . . .

SAMPLED: . . . . **RATING:** ☆☆☆☆☆

COLOR METER:

- MAHOGANY
- CARAMEL
- AMBER
- GOLD
- HONEY
- STRAW
- CLEAR

FLAVOR WHEEL:

HEAT/ABV : . . . . %

BALANCE
FINISH
BODY
DARK FRUIT
ASTRIN-GENT
CITRUS FRUIT
SALTY
FLORAL
SWEET
SPICY
SMOKE
HERBAL/GRASSY
PEAT
TOFFEE
MALT/CEREAL

0.1 0.2 0.3 0.4 0.5

NOTES:

. . . .

DISTILLER: ....

AGE/EXPRESSION: ....

ORIGIN: .... **PRICE:** ....

SAMPLED: .... **RATING:** ☆☆☆☆☆

COLOR METER:

- MAHOGANY
- CARAMEL
- AMBER
- GOLD
- HONEY
- STRAW
- CLEAR

FLAVOR WHEEL:

HEAT/ABV: _____ %

BALANCE · FINISH · DARK FRUIT · BODY · CITRUS FRUIT · ASTRINGENT · SALTY · FLORAL · SWEET · SPICY · SMOKE · HERBAL/GRASSY · PEAT · TOFFEE · MALT/CEREAL

0.5 / 0.4 / 0.3 / 0.2 / 0.1

NOTES:

....
....
....
....
....
....

DISTILLER: ....

AGE/EXPRESSION: ....

ORIGIN: .... **PRICE:** ....

SAMPLED: .... **RATING:** ☆☆☆☆☆

COLOR METER:

- MAHOGANY
- CARAMEL
- AMBER
- GOLD
- HONEY
- STRAW
- CLEAR

FLAVOR WHEEL:

HEAT/ABV: _____ %

BALANCE · FINISH · DARK FRUIT · BODY · CITRUS FRUIT · ASTRIN-GENT · SALTY · FLORAL · SWEET · SPICY · SMOKE · HERBAL/GRASSY · PEAT · TOFFEE · MALT/CEREAL

0.1 0.2 0.3 0.4 0.5

NOTES:

....

....

....

....

....

👉 **DISTILLER:** ....

AGE/EXPRESSION: ....

ORIGIN: .... **PRICE:** ....

SAMPLED: .... **RATING:** ☆☆☆☆☆

COLOR METER:

- MAHOGANY
- CARAMEL
- AMBER
- GOLD
- HONEY
- STRAW
- CLEAR

FLAVOR WHEEL:

HEAT/ABV: _____ %

BALANCE
FINISH
BODY
DARK FRUIT
ASTRIN-GENT
CITRUS FRUIT
SALTY
FLORAL
SWEET
SPICY
SMOKE
HERBAL/GRASSY
PEAT
MALT/CEREAL
TOFFEE

0.5 0.4 0.3 0.2 0.1

NOTES:

....
....
....
....
....
....

DISTILLER: . . . .

AGE/EXPRESSION: . . . .

ORIGIN: . . . . PRICE: . . . .

SAMPLED: . . . . RATING: ☆ ☆ ☆ ☆ ☆

COLOR METER:

MAHOGANY

CARAMEL

AMBER

GOLD

HONEY

STRAW

CLEAR

FLAVOR WHEEL:

HEAT/ABV : _____ %

BALANCE FINISH
BODY
ASTRIN-GENT   DARK FRUIT
SALTY   CITRUS FRUIT
SWEET   FLORAL
SMOKE   SPICY
PEAT   TOFFEE MALT/CEREAL HERBAL/GRASSY

0.5 0.4 0.3 0.2 0.1

NOTES:

. . . .

. . . .

. . . .

. . . .

. . . .

☞ DISTILLER:..

AGE/EXPRESSION:..................................

ORIGIN:.......................... PRICE:.............

SAMPLED:.......................... RATING: ☆☆☆☆☆

COLOR METER:

- MAHOGANY
- CARAMEL
- AMBER
- GOLD
- HONEY
- STRAW
- CLEAR

FLAVOR WHEEL:

HEAT/
ABV: _____ %

BALANCE FINISH

BODY

ASTRIN-
GENT

SALTY

SWEET

SMOKE

PEAT TOFFEE

MALT/
CEREAL

HERBAL/
GRASSY

SPICY

FLORAL

CITRUS
FRUIT

DARK FRUIT

0.5
0.4
0.3
0.2
0.1

NOTES:

....

....

....

....

....

....

👉 **DISTILLER:** ....

AGE/EXPRESSION: ....

ORIGIN: .... **PRICE:** ....

SAMPLED: .... **RATING:** ☆☆☆☆☆

COLOR METER:

- MAHOGANY
- CARAMEL
- AMBER
- GOLD
- HONEY
- STRAW
- CLEAR

FLAVOR WHEEL:

HEAT/ABV: _____ %

BALANCE · FINISH · DARK FRUIT · CITRUS FRUIT · FLORAL · SPICY · HERBAL/GRASSY · MALT/CEREAL · TOFFEE · PEAT · SMOKE · SWEET · SALTY · ASTRINGENT · BODY

0.1 0.2 0.3 0.4 0.5

NOTES:

....

....

....

....

....

....

DISTILLER: ....

AGE/EXPRESSION: ....

ORIGIN: .... PRICE: ....

SAMPLED: .... RATING: ☆ ☆ ☆ ☆ ☆

COLOR METER:

- MAHOGANY
- CARAMEL
- AMBER
- GOLD
- HONEY
- STRAW
- CLEAR

FLAVOR WHEEL:

HEAT/ABV: _____ %

BALANCE
FINISH
BODY
DARK FRUIT
ASTRIN-GENT
CITRUS FRUIT
SALTY
FLORAL
SWEET
SPICY
SMOKE
HERBAL/GRASSY
PEAT
TOFFEE
MALT/CEREAL

0.5 0.4 0.3 0.2 0.1

NOTES:

....

....

....

....

....

....

👉 **DISTILLER:** ....

AGE/EXPRESSION: ....

ORIGIN: .... **PRICE:** ....

SAMPLED: .... **RATING:** ☆ ☆ ☆ ☆ ☆

COLOR METER:

- MAHOGANY
- CARAMEL
- AMBER
- GOLD
- HONEY
- STRAW
- CLEAR

FLAVOR WHEEL:

HEAT/ABV: _____ %

BALANCE · FINISH · DARK FRUIT · CITRUS FRUIT · FLORAL · SPICY · HERBAL/GRASSY · MALT/CEREAL · TOFFEE · PEAT · SMOKE · SWEET · SALTY · ASTRINGENT · BODY

0.1 0.2 0.3 0.4 0.5

NOTES: ....
....
....
....
....
....